His Beauty Unveiled

Praise and Worship in Inspirational Poetry

By Anita K. Bube
a visual poetic artist

His Beauty Unveiled

Praise and Worship in Inspirational Poetry

By Anita K. Bube
a visual poetic artist

Home Crafted Artistry & Printing
New Albany, Indiana

Proudly printed and bound in the United States of America.
Cover photo by Carol Goodman Heizer, Louisville, KY

ISBN-13: 9-780 9827621-8-9
ISBN-10: 0-98276-21-8-6

Additional copies of this book may be purchased by visiting the E-Store for this title at: createspace.com/4184072

Home Crafted Artistry and Printing
1252 Beechwood Avenue
New Albany, IN 47150
e-mail: HomeCraftedArtistry@yahoo.com

Dedicated to My Mother,
Lillian May Taylor Blackman

I am now on the upper Spring of Mother's "Eternal Morning." Jesus took her home to live with Him on March 6, 2013. Mother graced this world with her irreplaceable love and her persevering presence for 91 years, 9 months and 7 days. I miss her dearly.

As I recall these nostalgic memories, God has graced the day this morning here on our 40+ acre farm with bright sunshine, blue sky and fluffy white clouds. Coincidently, I thought of Heaven. No more storm clouds for Mother!

When January 2013 arrived on God's calendar, as time is also in His hands, Mother's storm came suddenly. I didn't have the power to stop it. Mother's dementia worsened and it took an ugly turn. Before I realized the harm it brought, Jesus took Mother home. It was a whirlwind of care-giving. The Hosparus staff cared for her in her final hours. On that morning, "So sorry," pierced my soul and left a hole in my heart as deep as the ocean. My tears still flow as Mother sings Heaven's Eternal Song (she loved to sing). Mother is now healed. She is made whole.

I miss her friendship and love, deep and tender. She was a soft, meek, patient, humble, tranquil spirit. She will remain forever in the innermost room of my heart.

Mother daily read her Bible and leaned upon its promises through all her daily challenges. A loving portrait of a beautiful servant. Within her spirit God gave to her an "Aeolian Harp" which only God knew the tune and played it often to her soul. Through Mother's struggles (her illness) the most beautiful Heavenly Music was played to press her soul onward to something more wonderful. It was understood by her soul and sent on Angel wings.

Her role in life became mine as I took upon myself her struggles as her care-giver. They became my own to lay down at Jesus' feet. Both of us met many challenges and experienced many blessings and joys that I will continue to cherish with the ten years as her care-giver in our home. Through my care-giving of such a precious loving soul and spirit, God has given me more understanding. Mother helped me process the stages of our precious lives together.

First, I thank my Lord, Jesus Christ to whom I am a steward of His gifts and not owner of them. We should consecrate them to the Lord and make a commitment to use them in ways that honor God, that serve His purpose here. Secondly, I thank my beloved mother who lived that blessed life before me and left me a rich spiritual heritage.

Mother, 'til we meet again in Heaven,

Your Daughter,

Anita Karan

My Mother, Lillian May Taylor Blackman
May 27, 1921 – March 6, 2013

Table of Contents

Foreword 1

I have come to know the author, Anita K. Bube, and her husband, George Denzil, over the past five years, as their pastor. They have become friends of my family, and I believe she will be your friend, too, after you read her book, His Beauty Unveiled. Anita truly loves the Lord, and it shows in her life, in her soft-spoken words, and in her writings. I know her to be a caring and generous person who has the ability to bring poetry to life. She can paint a picture with her words. She can help you visualize her flower gardens and the countryside she knows and loves so well. Her words will inspire your soul. Each week I look forward to reading the poem she writes for our church bulletin. If you need refreshment, I recommend you treat yourself to her book of inspirational poetry and stories.

Dr. Rev. Cpt. Stephen E. Ellis, MSL CPCU, M. Div.
Former Pastor of The Lighthouse UMC,
Elizabeth, Indiana

Foreword 2

Beauty is one of the few common denominators running through all people groups in every language, clime, and period of history. Visual art, literature, and music play the heartstrings of the boorish and the civilized, the savage and the cultured, the pagan and the Christian. God has revealed Himself as an aesthetic God of exquisite beauty - through fields and flowers, mountain and stream, white water rapids and crystal cataracts, rainbows and sunsets, cloud formations by day and starry heavens by night, through morning sunbeams and evening moonlight. The human soul by nature resonates with beauty because it is incurably hungry for God.

With the stroke of an artist's brush, the author of this volume has dressed Christian truth with charming beauty, adorning exquisite concepts with God's own elegance. Anita K. Bube is uniquely qualified to do this because she herself is a beautiful soul. Throughout her life, she has continually been enriched by close association with Christ, daily feeding at God's table, and drinking from His Spirit. Through her dedicated talents, many persons have basked in God's presence and absorbed His ravishing beauty. That blessed experience awaits those who read this book.

Jon Tal Murphree
MA., M. Div., Litt. D.
(Currently residing in Toccoa, Georgia)

Foreword 3

I received an opportunity to meet the author of *His Beauty Unveiled* in 1995. After I received a diagnosis of multiple sclerosis, the Lord opened a ministry for me. At that time I had no idea that I would meet so many wonderful people that would stand with me through my difficulties as well as my blessings. One such beautiful person was Anita K. Bube. I met Anita while doing a gospel music concert in her hometown in Elizabeth, Indiana, at the Elizabeth UMC. She was sitting just a couple rows back. We had an immediate spiritual connection. She started writing me cards of encouragement after she learned I still had symptoms of the MS still remaining from my testimony. From time to time she tucked in a poem she had written. I soon invited her to go with me to minister. She opened with one or two beautiful poems before my concerts, and all were blessed. I suggested putting her poetry together in homespun booklets.

It has been a beautiful spiritual journey. I spoke encouragement back into her as she did for me when we first began together. She wrote in depth just as she walked deeper and more intimately with her Lord.

Recently, I went through a very rough time in my life, and I was hurting so much. She became my minister, feeding me the word of the Lord, and praying for me, and writing those beautiful love letters from God. Just as the Lord promised He would never leave nor forsake me, Anita never abandoned me in my hours of despair and need. I challenge each one of you who reads her book, *His Beauty Unveiled*, to allow yourself to find a quiet place, and bathe yourself in the Holy Presence of God. Enjoy the compilation of these beautiful love letters written in poetic meter: Anita's very own rhythmic verses inspired by God, autographed by the One she has loved and knows well, the Divine signature of her Saviour.

In His Divine Love –

Janet Rae Blosser
Associate of Arts in Biblical Studies
Gospel Music Singer and Composer

Acknowledgments

"He must become greater; I must become less"
John 3:30, NIV).

First and foremost, my desire is to serve Him. He became my Servant on the Cross of Calvary. I must give praise, honor, and glory to my sovereign Lord Jesus Christ. I am thankful He gave me a place of assurance to lay down my burdens at His feet! He has entrusted me with His gifts of encouragement. I am returning the blessings of His gifts by exalting His holy name, through my card ministry and poetry.

I couldn't have even begun this book without Michelle Thompson's generosity of her time and expertise. She said those four magic words, "I love to type." Thank you for putting up with my often-asked question, "How far are we?" I owe you a world of gratitude. I hope you know how much I thank God for your loyalty to me and to Him. I am eternally grateful to you.

"Thanks" to the many people through my card ministry who have said, "You need to share these words!" You are a blessing, and you have encouraged me.

Also to my monetary supporters: Earl & Ramona Beanblossom, and Tom and Janet Rae Blosser. Your blessings are also endless, and will help sow and reap eternal benefits. "Thanks" to Joyce Kintner who urged me in this direction. Person by person, God put people in my pathway to encourage me. She believed in me, although much life has happened in between the pages of this book. She gave me the confidence I needed to press onward. God sent her to me two years in advance to encourage me so I could stay focused, and not lose sight of my goal. An "indebted thanks" to John and Joyce Kintner for their gift of photography, and a shoulder to lean on. An "indebted thanks" also to Beverly Furnival for taking on this challenge for God's

18

Glory. I couldn't have done this without you. God placed you in my life at the exact time for His purpose and His Kingdom plan. I appreciate the extra miles you have walked beside me, and your unquestionable encouragement.

To God Be The Glory!

I am grateful to glean from the devotional books of Mrs. Charles Cowman (Lettie). She greatly inspired me, and has left a beautiful legacy to nurture many souls and spirits with her words of encouragement through inspirational poetry from authors she has selected and known from acquaintances, and also in her Divine Enlightenments and her short stories. I look forward to meeting her in heaven as we sit together to compare our notes.

Thank you to Carol Goodman Heizer for allowing me to use her lovely photograph for the front cover!

Also, much "thanks" to my hard-working Christian husband George Denzil for his "gift of tolerance" in finding an accumulated amount of ink pens and highlighters, yet still having a hard time finding the right one he needs at any given time. And for his "understanding nature" when seeing the old familiar scene of writing tablets, cards, stationery, devotionals, journals, commentaries, *Vine's* and *Strong's*, and *Webster* dictionaries, Bibles, and various other books scattered everywhere. For his "easy going nature" when I burned the midnight oil, searching for the meaning of a specific word or a divine inspiration in a line of poetry, or writing cards when the house was silent. Through the day he would often find me drawn aside from my domestic chores, sitting by Jesus' side, breathing in the relaxing Spirit of God that offers refreshment at His everlasting well.

19

Introduction

His Beauty Unveiled

"And the building of the wall of it was of jasper: and the city was pure gold, like unto clear glass. And the foundations of the wall of the city were garnished with all manner of precious stones. The first foundation was jasper; the second, sapphire; the third, a chalcedony; the fourth, an emerald. "
(Revelation 21:18, 19, *KJV)*

There's a story I'd like to share that runs parallel with the title of this book. Back in the 1990s God gave me a beautiful revelation. I accompanied my friend Janet Rae, a Gospel-singing artist, to the National Quartet Convention in Louisville, Kentucky a few times. She had rented a couple of booth spaces there. As an avid collector of fine costume and vintage jewelry for many years, she displayed and sold some exquisite pieces to well-known artists to help support her ministry. To preserve the jewelry in excellent condition, she transported them in Ziploc bags. To admire the true color and sparkling beauty of the stones, the bags were removed, and the jewelry displayed.

At that moment God gave me *His Beauty Unveiled.* God taught me through His Word and His Spirit of the beauty found within Himself. The gold reminded me of the scriptures I read about the streets of gold and the walls of jasper; the sapphire, emerald, garnet, amethyst, topaz, onyx, and many more precious stones.

Hallelujah! Alleluia!
To the Lamb of God!
Cast down your crowns
At His feet
And
Crown Him Lord of all!
Crown Him Lord of all!
Crown Him Lord of all!
Crown Him Lord of all!

*"And I saw no temple therein: for the Lord
God Almighty and the Lamb are the temple
of it. And the city had no need of the sun,
neither of the moon, to shine in it: for the
glory of God did lighten it, and the Lamb is
the light thereof."*

(Revelation 21:22, 23, KJV*)*

His Beauty
Unveiled

His Beauty Unveiled

...Heavenward...
My spirit is lifted
In holy reverence
Before the great I Am.

My soul is released
Into His healing hands.
I exalt You, 0 Consecrated Lamb.

As the radiance of Your Glory
Penetrates through the window of my soul,
It illuminates...
Creating in me
A beautiful part of You.

As the fresh winds of Your Spirit
Gently caress my soul,
We are on a sacred journey,
You...my Lord...and I
Embracing paradise.

We meet face to grace
Your beauty unveiled...sweet ambience,
Your sweet perfume,
O...holy fragrance.

Love in the First Degree

They lifted Me high
Against the angry sky....
My love for thee
Was imprinted upon Calvary's tree
By three rusty nails.
My love for thee is eternal: it will never fail...

THREE RUSTY NAILS — BLESSED TRINITY

Eternal Life you will inherit
When I come again...
To receive you unto Myself.
The "Crown of Thorns" they wreathed
And placed upon My feverish brow...
Will one day be your "Crown of Glory."

PRAISE HIS HOLY NAME!

They tore away My earthly raiment
And placed upon Me scarlet.
They mocked and hit Me, and in
Mockery they bowed down...
Then ... again they tore away My scarlet,
And placed upon Me My earthly raiment.
Soon I will be their sacrificial
Atonement for their sins.

GLORY TO THE KING OF KINGS!

My feet were bruised and bleeding
Upon the rugged road
So you, My redeemed, could walk
On streets of pure gold....

HALLELUJAH!
I was beaten and bruised and put to shame
So you, My dear children, could "Glorify My Name!"
Yes, I carried out my Father's will;
There was no guilt found in Me.
The only verdict I received was,

"LOVE IN THE FIRST DEGREE."

"However, when He, the Spirit of truth, has come,
He will guide you into all truth....
He will glorify Me,
for He will take of what is Mine
and declare it to you."
(John 16:13-14 NKJV)

PRAISE GOD!

"I am he that liveth, and was dead; and, behold, I am
alive for evermore, Amen; and have the keys of hell and
of death."
(Revelation 1:18, KJV)

Again...I Walk

Again...I walk through the valley;
I sense the presence of my Lord so sweetly;
I focus on His compassionate face.
From His heart He gives to me
His infinite mercy and grace.

Through my valley I've seen a glorious light,
For I know that Jesus walks before me;
He clears my difficult path, and places a rose
Where the thorns grow.

I don't mind the valleys anymore,
For Jesus and I are dearest friends.
He understands my pain,
And I learn more of Him....

Climbing a Mountain

I'm climbing a mountain –
Hardships seem so many:
I go up one step,
And I'm knocked down by two.

If I could just step somewhere firmly
Without the sinking sand,
I know I shall make it,
Holding onto God's strong hand.

If I could see the grass so green
Instead of parched land,
If I could just see a ray of sun
Instead of the dark night,

If I could just grasp onto hope,
I know everything will be all right.

When I see the cord of faith to climb
That mountain to the top,
I know God's love will get me through.
Jesus has gone on before and prepared the way.

He has weaved the cord of perseverance
To help me up above it all.
My soul shall sing a full chorus of Hallelujahs
And praise to my Lord, for He is always with me
When things are really hard.

Caring for Me

Lord, care for me as I walk through the storm.
As the winds come upon me, walk with me through it
All.

Hold my hand and help me stand
When doubts and fears come upon my soul,
Lord, help me to be in control.
Give to me the faith to fight the battle and hope as
My Shield.

Provide me with Your divine strength to do Thy will;
Bind me with Your great love, and give me Your peace
That flows like a fountain.

I know I can't always be on top of heaven's mountain,
For I can look beyond and see the valleys I must
Walk through.
But it doesn't matter anymore,
For I know You.

Tears at Calvary

Mary, the mother of Jesus–
Can we feel her pain ...
As her beloved Son hung on
Calvary's cross?
Can we see her tears flow
Down her face in disbelief?

Can we feel her heart full of
Terrifying pain
As Jesus' blood fell on
Calvary's hill –
That sacred ground on which Mary
Stood,
The Holy Ground that held that
Rugged, hewn cross –

Can Mary's tears be forgotten?
Will the cruel cross that held
That ultimate Sacrifice always
Be remembered?
Are we "rejoicing" with Mary,
As her Son (Our Precious Lord) holds
The key to eternal life in His
Hands?

That once broken body –
Is now our Great Physician,
The Healer of all mankind.
"Jesus Lives," the
Crimson sacrifice for our
Sins.
Everlasting life – Eternally His!!!

The Ascension

Open, ye deaf ears, and hear the
Trumpet of our Lord:
Here He comes the King of kings,
Our Majesty!
He is the great I Am –
the Alpha, the Omega.
Yes – it is He.

Leap for joy, ye lame,
For you will know no more sorrow
Or pain –
Behold, ye blind, for now you see
The One who died for thee.

Leave behind your worry and care,
For today Jesus is meeting you
In the air.
Forget about your frets and fears,
For Jesus has come, He is here!

No need to worry about tomorrow
Or yesterday,
For you have left behind the
Time to pray.

Forget about the things you just had to do,
For you've made reservations to
Eternity.
Your home in heaven has been pre-approved;
No further ado – there's nothing left to say,
But to tell you I've been waiting
For this glorious day!!

I'm One Step Closer

One step closer I am,
One step closer after the storm.
Oh, the wind that rages,
How furious the gale!
I know my Lord – will prevail!

Oh, precious is the hope
That calms the storm.
He is my Rock of Ages;
He saves me from all harm.

No matter how furious the storm
Or how much this ship is battered,
I will put up my sail, though
Worn and tattered,
For Jesus is the Master of the sea.

Oh, how wonderful the calm;
Oh, how marvelous His sweet assurance,
Knowing that Jesus goes with me
Through it all – safe and secure,
I'm just one step closer:
His love so wonderful endures!

O Cross of Golgotha

O rugged cross of Golgotha,
How dare you stand so sturdy
To hold this precious One
That is so pure and holy –

O rugged cross,
You caused my Lord great pain,
You held those nails so tightly;
Your purpose – your Heavenly Father knew –
It was eternal life to gain –

O rugged cross,
Why did you weigh so heavy upon
His bleeding back?
Bruised – Scorned – Rejected –
Why did you crucify this innocent Man?

Why didn't you heed His cry,
Causing Him to drink that bitter
Cup of agony?
O bloodstained cross,
Have you no remorse –

Were you there when they crucified my Lord?

The Highest Bidder

An auctioneer stands before us:
He starts the bid – "What will you give for this soul,
Fifty to a hundred or so. Who will start the bid?"
In the midst of the crowd stands a kind
And gentle Man.
He breaks the silence, and listens to the
Cry of the auctioneer.
He kindly nods his head with a look
Of compassion, and He bids on this precious soul:

"I will give him eternal life
Far more valuable than gold.
I was bought with thirty pieces of silver;
I hung on the cross for all mankind.
I paid for him that "day"
With My precious blood that was shed
Upon Calvary's tree; he was cleansed and set free –

"My debt I've paid to society",
Stamped on the eternal pages.
My 'Amazing Grace' echoes through the
Changing times.
I am the' Solid Rock' upon which you stand;
I am there...still your heart, and listen to Me.
I change not – I am forever the same;
I led one solitary life; I died and arose again.
My name is Eternal, for I am Jesus –
Alpha and Omega – The Beginning and the End."

In Him I have all things.

On the Wings of Prayer

On the wings of prayer:
Oh, what a heavenly thought!
Soared on high before His throne,
Our sins through His blood He bought.
Yes, through the fluffy white clouds
Into the heaven beyond:
My Saviour is there.
Although I do not see His face,
In His presence I'm in a holy place.
From His throne above
Comes hope, peace, and love.
I do not ask for riches on this earth,
Nor anything fancy and such –
I just want His nail-scarred hand to touch
Me – when I'm weary and tired.
And when the winds of doubt and fear
Come upon my heart,
I just want to feel Him,
His presence so dear.
I look into the heavens,
And I yearn to see
The One who loves me and
Died for me –
Yes, Jesus bore my sins on Calvary's tree.
It was there He set me free:
Free from the bars of bondage,
Free from the strife within.
On an angel's beautiful wings
Our prayers soar high,
For Jesus waits for us there,
Somewhere up there past
The clouds in the sky.

Perfect–Imperfect

*"There is no fear in love; but perfect love casteth out
fear: because fear hath torment. He that feareth is
not made perfect in love.
We love him, because he first loved us."
(1 John 4:18, 19, KJV)*

I look at a rose, and I see how flawless the delicate petals.
I focus on myself, and see within myself imperfections, but
A soul (mind, will, and emotions) patterning my life after
My Lord. Although the road of life is unstable at times,
I can look up and feel Him walking so sweetly beside me.
In Him I have strength for this day, and through Him
I have His grace for tomorrow.
In Him I have "all" things.
Glory to His name.

Visions of His Glory

AAAHHH ... The sweet fragrance
In the sanctuary of His Spirit
I can just smell ... His sacred aroma.
Oh ... how beautiful He flows ... through ... me!
Oh ... how awesome His ... beauty!

Oh ... the beauty You impart!
Your spirits ... fire ...
Your ... desire.

Oh ... I cannot fathom ...
The depth ...
Nor the height ...

Nor the breadth ...
Nor the length ...
Of Your great and mighty
Love and Power.
Ephesians 3:18

Through the fullness of Your Spirit
Engrave ... Your image within ... me.
I exalt Your everlasting name! !
I bow ... down before the King of Kings.
Behold!! ... I hear the hymns of Your praises

Ring ...
Throughout Your eternity.
You are the Heir of all things ...
You are my Dayspring ...
You are the Sustaining Bread in my life ...
You are the Morning Star.

Hebrews 1:2
Luke1
John 6:35
Revelation 22:16

Jesus – I Finally Made It

After the thunder there comes the rain
Through all the trials,
Through all the pain –
I've made it through it all with Jesus.

After the storm there comes the calm –
Through all the tribulations,
Through valleys deep and wide –
I've made it through with Jesus by my side.

After the rain there comes the flowers –
Tears bring forth strength;
Strength brings forth faith;
Faith brings forth power –
I've made it through, Sweet Jesus.

I've made it through to Your reaching arms;
I've felt Your warm and gentle embrace;
I've felt the tears from Your face –
Fall on mine.

Need not a word be spoken – only the
Flutter of angels' wings,
For I have made it Home to heaven;
My soul will forever sing –
HALLELUJAH!

I was studying a portrait of Jesus hugging a dear child of God who had made it home to Him. They are dressed in white robes, standing in fluffy clouds. I felt the emotions of Jesus as did the artist. I saw the tender mercies of my Lord that day as He was weeping.
"For the Lamb which is in the midst of the throne shall feed them, and shall lead them unto living fountains of waters: and God shall wipe away all tears from their eyes."
(Revelation 7:17, KJV)

Springs of Praise

Oh...shall I see through Thine eyes
The glory revealed for me?
With a waiting heart I surpass to see
Thy great majesties.

"He makes springs pour water into the ravines;
It flows between the mountains."
(Psalm 104:10, NIV)

Even through life's diseases
You shall set our spirits free;
You shall give to...me
Your springs of peace.

Oh...Living Water,
Fountain of everlasting life –
Oh... springs of eternal hope
Flow through the veils of the night.

Oh...come to me as Your
Spring of refuge
Through the valleys of my soul.
Oh...come, Holy Spirit,
Making me eternally whole.

Oh...come...Holy Spring of praise:
Encircle me with Your garlands of love
As a sacred garment enrobing my spirit
From the grandeur of heaven above.

A Servant's Prayer

Lord ... sometimes it is so hard
To walk on this journey:
The pain ... is so great,
And I ... so frail.

But I know ... by holding
Onto Your mighty hand,
You ... will walk with me
And be my Friend.

Your promises help me to endure,
And they will never fail.
"... *I am with you always ...*"
(Matthew 28:20, NKJV)

You know the heart of "me,"
And you know the times
I really ... must lean
So very ... much.

Thank You, Lord, ...
for being with me,
Right ... where I am,
For I know ... You ... understand.

Your sacrifice on the cross of Calvary
Was for "me":
You took upon yourself
My infirmities.

"He took up our infirmities and carries our diseases."
(Matthew 8:176, NIV)

Yes ... Lord, although I have struggles,
It is in my weakness
I've felt Your strength,
And by your mighty hand

You shall guide
... me ...
To our VICTORIES.

Praise God for His unending mercy!

A Broken Vessel Made Whole

God chose me,
An earthen vessel,

And He places the pieces
Ever so gently upon the potter's wheel.

He begins to fashion me
Through the storm of my trials
... My valleys ...

With the tears from my soul,
A broken vessel begins to be made whole.

I lay upon the potter's wheel
Like a lump of clay in the Master 's hands.

With His compassion He feels
Each lump of pain
And each hidden flaw.
As I began yielding to Him my all,

With a loving touch
He molds His will into mine.
Oh...sweet surrender!
Oh...holy sacrifice!

There are times when I don't
Understand.
In those moments –
He holds me so
Very close and tenderly

As He continues to mold
Into...me...His Divine plan.

I am a broken vessel willing
To be made whole.

Holding Me Through the Night

Come...O Lord...
I seek Your holy face;
Surround me with Your arm's embrace.

As prayers rise
To Thy majestic throne,
Hold my hand...
For you are the "Mighty One."

Come...O Lord...
And lead the way
Through my darkest hour,
For only the "Holy One" can guide me
Through this storm.

Peace then filled my heart,
And I knew...
That the "Mighty One" had
Brought me through.

"I'll never leave you,"
Said a Voice so clear and tenderly
As I awoke from my night's sleep.

This was written when my husband was facing surgery. Indeed, God is our Lily in our valleys. His presence is evident in the sweet peace and hope that follow our prayers.

Celestial Perfume

(Prayer)

O Holy Garment of Prayer,
O holy baptism from the sapphire throne,
O Divine elegance –
God's shekinah grace,
O Majestic bridge,
A balsam for my soul, Hallelujah!

O prayer's sweet perfume
Coming down from heaven's ethereal room –
O fragrant incense
Falling as celestial dust
Upon my breast,
Rise up in me your artesian well,
Always full and overflowing
With prayer's sweet perfume.

"Of Him my meditation shall
Sweet thoughts to me afford,
and as for me, I will rejoice
in God, my only Lord."
(Psalm 104:34)

Exalt the Name of Jesus!

Exalt the name of Jesus:
My knees prostrate fall!
Exalt the name of Jesus:
He is Lord of all!

"This is how God showed his love among us:
He sent his one and only Son into the world
that we might live through Him"
(1 John 4:9, NIV)

Exalt His name
Through my afflictions
And through my pain,
For through them all
Treasures from heaven I will attain.

"I am a rose of Sharon,
a lily of the valleys."
(Song of Solomon 2:1, NIV)

Exalt His Name!
You are the "King of who I am,"
O...Yahweh...Rophe,
God's unblemished Holy Lamb.

Exalt His name!
To heaven's heights
I am yours, and you are Mine.
Exalt His name!
"I am the true vine,
...and...
my Father is the gardener."
(John 15:1, NIV)

"...It is my Father who gives you the true bread from heaven. For the bread of God is he who comes down from heaven and gives life to the world."
(John 6:32, 33, NIV. Also read verses 48·50.)

Only To Touch the Hem of His Garment

Scriptures: Matthew 9:20-22; 14:35, 36

Just enough faith in Him to believe
That while in His presence
His healing to receive.

O dear one, we need to cling to Him,
And wholeheartedly lean on His mighty arms,
Trusting, leaning, protecting us
From life's surpassing storms.
Reach out...
For hope and redeeming grace
As you touch the hem of His garment.
In this holy place, you shall be touched
By His consuming fire,
Set free through His healing power,
Purified from all fears and all doubts:
An Ecclesiastes time of deliverance!
Hallelujah!

He knows each time
We call out His mighty name;
His mercy endures forever,
Down through the ages:
He will never change!

He weaves a new garment
From the cleansing of each thread
Stained from within:
A covering of forgiveness,

A cloak of worthiness,
A new garment for an overcomer
Receiving this purging power.

My desire is to constantly seek after Him and to know
Him in greater length and depth, cleansing me from
all unrighteousness, so I will be worthy to stand
before His throne.

A Promise

I looked around and saw the homes, without lights
Because of the snowstorm. A feeling of bleakness came
Over my soul. I happened to catch a glimpse of the glorious
Sunset almost gone from sight. I felt the cold of the snow
Melting slowly underneath a brilliance of
White.
I felt alone with a tinge of silent frustration,
But I was not alone, for Jesus is always with me.
He brings sunlight to my soul:
The light that overcomes darkness.

During the storm I heard the song of a bird –
The promise of spring – of life anew.
Jesus said, "Lo, I am with thee, even unto the
End of the world." How bleak is our world without
Jesus! Will you leave this world with Him?
Believe in His promise today, and thou shalt be saved.

His Name is Wonderful!

The Staff of His Mercy

O affliction that heals –

After the storm a rainbow yields –
After the plough –
A planted – flow'r.

In the blackest of night
An angel's presence –
A glint of celestial white –

O thorns that pierce my soul,
This, too, shall pass,
For they have no power over me –
I hold within my heart
Heaven's harp,
Hallelujahs' everlasting jubilee –

From the gale of the night
Cometh forth joyous singing –
From the shore
Cometh forth ringing
Of heaven's bells.

"When thou passeth through the waters, I will be with thee; And through the rivers, they shall not overflow thee: When thou walkest through the fire, thou shalt not be burned: Neither shall the flame kindle upon thee."
    (Isaiah 43:2, KJV)

Abba, Father

Who's going to hold me

When I cry,
And wipe these tears
From my eyes? –

Abba, Father.
Come and be my consolation.

Come and hold my heart,
Hold it sooo very tight,
'til I come through the
Veil of this night –

Abba, Father.
Come and be my Hope.

Quiet my soul
As though –
I am an empty cup
Waiting to be filled
With your Spirit.

Take my hand,
Leading me in Your footsteps .
After Thee my soul
Panteth
For Thy holy will.

Take Thou my heart:
It is my desire
For Thee to fulfill.

*"As the deer panteth for the water brooks,
So pants my soul for You, O God."
(Psalm 42:1, NKJV)*

In Love and Devotion:
"The Royal Candle"

Radiantly He shines through the window of my soul.
Silently and gloriously the essence
Of His presence descends around me.
I am captivated by His "Holy" Spirit.
I stand in stillness as His promises are revealed.
I am facing His throne that is covered
By a veil because "The Royal Candle"
Is so bright and beautiful, I cannot look upon Him.
It's like I am frozen in time, and nothing else matters
But the things that are between my Lord and me.
He is my "Royal Candle" who shines in
The darkness, dispelling the gloom.
By day and by night He is my watchtower.
He protects, He loves, He secures. I am kept in
"The hollow of His hand," the deep place in
His hand where I am restored and renewed
Day by day. He is my "Hiding Place"
To protect me from trouble, a place that
Surrounds my soul with the "Song of Deliverance."
When the storms of life are raging,
I am kept in the "hollow of His hand,"
Where the "Royal Candle" shines upon me.
Praise my Lord! I am secure in my "Hiding Place,"
A place where His love keeps me warm.

Recently, I purchased perennials called "The Royal Candle." Their royal purple spikes seem to be reaching upward towards their Creator, praising Him. I call my flower garden, "God's Victory Garden" because He created everything uniquely beautiful: all the tiny details are His signature of authenticity.

56

We are inheritors into the Kingdom through His blood. We are His sons and daughters adopted in the line of royalty in His Kingship.

"You are my hiding place;
you will protect me from trouble
and surround me with songs of deliverance."
(Psalm 32: 7, NIV)

"However, we possess this precious treasure [the divine light of the Gospel] in [frail human] vessels of earth, that the grandeur and exceeding greatness of the power may be shown to be from God and not from ourselves."
(2 Corinthians 4:7, Amp.)

If I Only Had Wings

"Oh that I had wings like a dove!
For then would I fly away,
and be at rest."
(Psalm 55:6, KJV)

When my soul and spirit becomes weary,
I want to escape –
To my Hiding Place.

I shall hide in Thy bosom, 0 Lord,
For You are my Refuge,
My Secret Sanctuary.

The Breath of your Spirit
Gives me courage to press through
The wind and the storm.
Your hands are faithful,

and I know
They purposely guide –
Though my battles are pressing in
On every side.
Your love is like a beacon
That shines through the darkness
Of my night.

You are my Dwelling Place
Where storms eventually cease.
A place where You gently
Restore and faithfully lead.

No one fully understands
But You, my Heavenly Father, Friend.

Always
And
Forever
Hold to my changing hand.

*"I would hasten my escape
from the windy storm and tempest."
(Psalm 55:8, KJV)*

That I Might Know the Father's Heart

My desire is to know the Father's heart. The desire
Flows into an ongoing craving within my inner being.
*"Blessed are the poor in spirit: for theirs is the
kingdom of heaven."   (Matthew 5:3, KJV)*

To be "poor in spirit" is to totally depend on God.
To depend upon God is to let him be the sole Proprietor
Of your life. We must believe and realize we are totally
Blind and helpless. We must believe we need the grace
Of God for the very first glimmer of light to acquire the
Fullness of His grace. We must turn away from all forms
Of pride, self reliance, all confidence, self assurance,
And all self-sufficiency.

One day I had a lot of questions as my
Body fell under the threat of an illness. I leaned
Toward the wisdom of medical specialists while
Also trusting through my days of waiting that my
"Great Physician" was holding and healing me
Through this trying time.

There were times when I simply wanted to be left
Alone, alienated from people, and to be with just Jesus.
As I stood standing in the midst of my discouragement,
I also felt God's hand of encouragement
Pressing me forward,
Toward something "more wonderful and beautiful"
As He teaches me more of the things He is.
More of knowing the Father's heart,
And spiritually visioning the beauty of His soul and spirit.
I testified of God's healing. My goal is to know Him.
Perhaps there is nothing more comforting than to realize
That Jesus knows me already. He knows me inside and out...

And He loves me still. We need to search
Our own hearts and pour out to Him,
To the One who begs for you to know Him.
I am striving to do what Paul speaks of in
Philippians 3:10 *(NKJV)*. He says,

*"That I may know Him and the power of His resurrection,
and the fellowship of His sufferings,
being conformed to His death."*

I seek to progressively become more
Deeply and intimately acquainted with Him,
Perceiving, recognizing, and understanding the
Wonders of His person more strongly and more clearly,
That I may know the "power" overflowing
From "His Resurrection," and that I may so share
His suffering as to be "continually transformed"
In spirit into "His likeness," even to "His death"
And, "His hope."

The Best Is Yet To Come

When you are wounded and
Brokenhearted,
Remember,
Your soul was created in His Image.
He understands –
He is
Your Shelter, Hope, and Strength.
He has your life in the hollow of His hands –

The best is yet to come.

When you are in your darkest storm,
And night covers your world,
He is the "Lamp" that guides you,
And the Light that guards your way.
He will teach you how to "trust" Him;

He has saved the best for last.

Silver or gold have I none –
But I am laying treasures in
Heaven's storehouse.
The best is yet to come –
There is a realm of Glory,
Unseen and unknown,
Where God is working things out
We cannot see –

Someday
The mysteries of His great love
Will be unveiled,
And we
Shall see Him
As He is:
The Lord of Lords
And the
King of Kings –

Hallelujah!
Sing Praises to the Lamb of God!

Holding Me

When you feel like there's no other
Place but
To crawl up into the sweet arms of
Jesus,
Remember,
He was the One who held you first:
He stroked your brow
With His compassion,
And called you by name.
You are His child –

When the road seems rough,
And there's not enough
Love flowing through,
Remember,
God loved you first.
When love is tough, and it hurts –

When you feel like you are tossed
About,
And the enemy is after your soul –
Remember
Who loved you first ... He knows

When you hurt so bad,
And you can't find even a note of a
Song
To sing yourself through –
Remember,
By trusting in Him He'll make
Things different ...
All things new.

When your eyes are swollen with
Tears,
Remember,
Your pain is His to bear.
He knows and He cares;

He will lift your burden to Calvary:
No dearer place to call our own,
No dearer place to call home.

In His Unlimited Grace,
Mercy, and Love

*In the summer of 2009, a friend of mine was going through "her darkest nights." Thus the poems "*The Best Is Yet To Come*" and "*Holding Me*" were inspired by the Holy Spirit. The words brought comfort to her. She always knew that God was leading and protecting her.*

No Higher Calling

No higher calling (1 Corinthians 7:22)

Than to be a free servant of God,

Partakers of the heavenly calling (Hebrews 3:1),

Continually pressing toward the cross,
Walking in His righteousness alone.

Chosen by God – purposeful plan.

I know it pleases You, Father,
When we accept Your spiritual gifts
Full and free –
I feel You dance in the spirit,
And You laugh, gleefully.

Imagine how God feels
When He gives you a gift
From His heart,
And it is left on the shelf of your life

Unopened! Forgotten!

What's beyond God's bow of mercy
But enduring faith, amazing love,
And eternal hope;
What's beyond that special gold wrapping
But the Bread of Life
Just waiting to fill you
And feed your soul.

What's inside for you
But God's heart
He wants to give away.
Through His gifts we honor Him,
And give back the eternal treasures
He has given us.
It was He who set us free –
To choose.

Delight thyself in God; He'll give
Thine heart's desire to thee.
(Psalm 37:4)

It is my heart's desire to serve. Blessed as I have been
to serve others – you have served and blessed me
through your smiles and greetings and the sharing of
the encouragement of our Lord Jesus Christ. We are
His tools in His hands. He is the greatest Healer to
all. Daily I strive to live in His image – to be the
reflection He calls me to be through His Holy
Countenance.

Serving The King of Glory!

You Light Up My Life

As I sit by my window,
I am reminded of Your sovereign power.
After the barren season,
Underneath the winter snow,
Awaits a seed to blossom:
Your promise of resurrected hope.

The wind breathes, and upon it
The song of birds and their praise
Whether in sunshine or rain,
You light up my life,
And give me hope to carry on.

As the morning sun comes shining through
Radiant rays of Your undying love
Assures me I do not walk alone,
I am surrounded by Your Holy Presence.
You rejoice over me with love's unending song;
You give me hope to carry on.

"He waters the mountains from his upper chambers."
(Psalm 104:13a, NIV)
And watereth my soul as well.
All my springs of joy are in Him.

'O give praise and thanks to the Lord
For bountiful is He.
His tender mercy doth
'Endure unto eternity. "
(Psalm 106:1)

He gives me prisms of precious promises,
And fills my nights with His song.
You light up my life and give me
Strength and hope to carry on.

"The LORD your God is with you
He is mighty to save.
He will take – great delight in you,
He will quiet you with his love,
He will rejoice over you with singing ".
(Zephaniah 3:17, NIV)

"For with you is the fountain of life;
In Your light we see light."
(Psalm 36:9, NASB)

The song "You Light Up My Life" was the inspiration
for this poem. Truly my Jesus is my Song through the
day and through the night.

All Praise To His Holy Name!

The Song Within

Never a sore trial
That God is not in it:
Even in the valleys
He is there
To bring you through –
He'll transform your place of darkness
Into heaven – just for you.

He sings over me the song of consolation.

The load I carried
Seemed so much to bear –
I cried out and He answered *(Isaiah 58:9)*.
He took me to the cross
My burden was lifted there –

He sings with me the song of victory!

In the midst of my storms
He is my Hiding Place.
Hallelujah!
From His seat of Mercy
He anchors my soul
And gives me His sweet peace
Over my troubled waters.

He sings to me the song of deliverance.

In the darkness of night,
In the middle of pain
O Lord, You are sovereign;
Thy Holy Name sustains –

You sing to me Your song of rapturing hope.

I know the music of His soul
Is always with me.
Through all my fiery trials
He is my merciful King –

We sing together the songs of praise.

"I will sing unto the LORD as long as I live:
I will sing praise to my God while I have my being."
(Psalm 104:33, KJV)

God does not waste our pain. Never believe we walk
alone on this earthly journey. He feels our pain we
bear; He knows our sorrows. No one wants a cross to
bear, but they often come. Many things about
tomorrow I don't seem to understand, but I know my
Heavenly Father holds my hand. My journey is
presently here, but my Heart is eternally there where
He is.

Filled With Hope

In His Shadow

In His shadow He washes my eyes
With His tears.
His compassion fails me not;
His mercies are new every morning.
(Lamentations 3:22, 23).

I am His child;
He draws me near
And shelters me by His side.
As His child
I will still have trials

He hides me in the shadow of His wings (Psalm 17:8),

And give me strength to soar –
With the breath of His Spirit
He lifts me higher
Than I've ever been before –
Hallelujah!

He is my Shadow (Isaiah 32:2),

My Sanctuary in the desert,
My Eternal Spring,
My Living Water,
Refreshing my soul.

A servant desires the shadow (Job 7:2a):

A place of refuge,
A place of encouragement,
To endure the journey –
A place to persevere in time of storm.
Hallelujah!

In the shadow of the cross
We are bathed in His presence,
Empowered by His love,
Cleansed by His blood.
Hallelujah!

The shadow of Christ is a place of refuge for the weary, a place to hold us in His arms, strength for our journey, trust in His direction, joy to lighten our load, His peace to comfort us, His hope to persevere in times of trial, His cloak of protection through storms. God always has a purpose and a plan through our trials. We don't just go through them without a result, or His purpose being fulfilled. He always has so much, much more to give. God will not withhold anything of Himself from His children. In our places of hardship, sorrow, and fiery trials He gives us totally His all. He never fails us nor forgets us nor leaves us. "...Lo, I am with you always...." (Matthew 28:20, NKJV).

Through His Grace Always

I Shall Return

The day of the Lord shall come
As a thief in the night.
He will come and gather up all
Who believe in His name,
Escorting us to heaven, forever
With Him to reign.

We must follow in His footsteps,
Keeping watch with lamps burning bright.
Victoriously, His mighty army marches nigh.
Be prepared as the King of Glory
Blows His trumpet across
The Eastern sky!

Hallelujah!

We cannot comprehend all the
Things He has prepared.
Many mansions as He has said
From prophecies foretold,
Written by God's own Hand.

When His message of salvation is not heeded,
What a day of regrets that will be,
When we didn't spare the time to hear
Those eternal words of Life that
Fell upon deaf ears.

"O sinner, repent," as John the Baptist exhorted,
For surely you will stand
Before Him when the Book of your Life
Is opened before His heavenly courts one day.
God gives us an escape from the gates of hell
In the cleansing power through the
Blood of the Lamb!

Hallelujah!

God gave us the one sacrifice of
His only beloved Son,
A signature required from heaven,
Stamped and sealed by His
Nail-scarred hands.

"Then I looked and heard the voice of many angels, numbering thousands upon thousands, and ten thousand times ten thousand. They encircled the throne and the living creatures and the elders. In a loud voice they sang: 'Worthy is the Lamb, who was slain, to receive power and wealth and wisdom and strength and honor and glory and praise!' Then I heard every creature in heaven and on earth and under the earth and on the sea, and all that is in them, singing: 'To him who sits on the throne and to the Lamb be praise and honor and glory and power, forever and ever!' The four living creatures said 'Amen,' and the elders fell down and worshiped."
(Revelation 5:11-14, NIV)
Read Revelation 7, and especially focus on verses 13-17.
Receive God's blessed promises.

Hallelujah, to the Lamb of God!

Just Inside Heaven's Gate

O sweet release –
Crossing over to the other side
Forever with Jesus to abide,
Resting in His unchanging Grace,
Someday I'll stand with Him face to face.
I'll be there at the Eastern gate.
I'll be waiting for you there –
Brother, sister, friend.
O jubilant day!
Where the joys of heaven have no end.
Oh, to see what I now see:
Heaven's bliss!
You wouldn't waste a moment
To accept His wondrous love.
In His presence is fullness of joy.
Like me you'll take your wings and
Fly away as the snow white dove.
Now I am free!
For a time my body was
Weighed down with disease.
Why not be glad for me?
I am Home now. I am free!
Rejoice with me!
I'll be looking for you
Just inside the Eastern gate.

The Holy Spirit gave me affirmations that day. The chosen sympathy card had the very scene of Jesus praying in the garden as the stained glass window portrayed above their brother's casket. The Bible verse that I had written in the card was the same one shared at the end of the sermon. Their brother had seen Jesus the day before he went home to heaven. His journey was made complete that day. As we departed I whispered in their ears, "You'll see him again!" What a consolation to know God keeps His promises. That day is ours to hold in eternal hope. God's blessed assurance for His saints.

'You will show me the path of life [the resurrection]; In Your presence is fullness Joy: At Your right hand are pleasures forevemore. " (Psalm 16:11, NKJV)

In Memory of William "Bill" Bube - Brother-in-Law May 31, 1934 – May 3, 2008

Imagine Meeting Him

Just imagine meeting Him:
His Heavenly Glory,
Our guilt and shame,
And know the power of His Holy Presence,
And in His Holy Name.

Imagine Him walking with you,
Brother to brother, son, daughter, friend,
A Holy Communion that will never end.

Jesus, "Wonderful Counselor, Mighty God"
(Isaiah 9:6)

Imagine meeting Him
Face to face
Because He has chosen you
To be His Eternal Light
In a world of morally and spiritually dark places.

"I am the Light of the World"
(John 8:12)

Imagine Him dying for you:
The Broken Bread in the upper room,
The Blood Covenant poured out,
The empty tomb.

Golgotha's Unblemished "Lamb of God"
(John 1:29)

Imagine meeting Him in the resurrection.
While hell shuddered,
All heaven and nature sang
To His faithful followers.
Freedom reigned:
The certificate of debt was torn in two,
Giving us glorious victory over sin and the grave.

Hallelujah- Hallelujah-Hallelujah!!

"I am the Alpha and Omega, the beginning and the end"
(Revelation 21:6)

And "The Resurrection and the Life"
(John 11:25)

Calvary, Our Crown of Glory

O Lily of the Valley,
To those whose trials are long and sore
You carry upon Your shoulder our sorrows,
Illuminating, as the morning sun,
A pathway to heaven's open door.

O Rose of Sharon,
A scarlet flower of Israel's plains,
A sacred blossom crushed by sorrow,
Grief, and pain,
Heaven's holy fragrance.

A cry rang out through
Gethsemane's Garden that day.
He obediently yielded to His Father's will
"Not My will, but Thine, be done."
The cry pierced His Father's heart
As He held to His bosom
His one and only beloved Son.

O Blessed Redeemer,
You endured it all for me,
Weeping, sobbing, bitterly.
O bitter myrrh mingled with pure love's
Sovereign sacrifice
Sacred tears – holy ground
Beneath the olive trees.
O sweet victory
In Gethsemane's cup of agony.

In every Calvary there is a blossom,
In every shadow an abiding light,
In every desert a flower blooming.
After the cross, Calvary blossoms
With resurrected Glory:
Our inheritance of eternal life.

My All for Him

*"Then spake - Jesus again unto them, saying, I am the light
of the world: he that followeth me shall not walk
in darkness, but shall have the light of life."
(John 8:12, KJV)*

My all for Him:
Nothing less,
Only Jesus
And His righteousness.

My all for Him:
As I journey with "The Light of my world,"
Yes, Lord, sometimes faltering in this flesh,
But standing strong
While Satan's darts at me are hurled.

My all for Him:
To praise and breathe His holy name,
To come into His holy place.
Before you, O Great I Am,
I come face to grace.

My all for Him:
His Spirit flowing through my soul,
His love through my hands,
His mercy extended without demand.

My all for Him:
His daughter without request;
My beloved King
In everything,
He gives me His very best.

The Bread of Life

O Lord, sometimes I am so ashamed
To even call out Your holy name!
How patient You've been to me,
How merciful Your grace!

When I am afflicted in spirit
My faith in You does not fail.
Your awesome love always will lift me;
You've taught me how to stand with You
Through each and every stormy gale.

You've sifted me like grains of wheat;
I've felt Your consuming fire within me;
Like chaff my sins fell away.
While I was lying on the thresher's floor
You gathered me up again and helped me
Stand,
For You require the purest of grain
As a sacrificial offering to serve Thee humbly.
At Your blessed feet

You've crushed me, my Lord,
As grain to the mill.
With Your hands of perseverance
You mold me into the perfect design of Your
Holy will.

Oh, may the fresh winds of Your Spirit
Blow away the chaff until all is left
A holy aroma by fire –
Thy Holy Bread of Life.

"For the bread of God is he who comes down from heaven and gives life to the world ... . I am the bread of life ... ."
(John 6:33, 35, NKJV)

This poem originated through one of Beth Moore's studies entitled "Jesus, the One and Only" taught by Linda Stewart at First Baptist Church in the fall of 2007. There was a segment entitled, "Sifted Like Wheat." At the beginning of each DVD lesson a blending of English and Hebrew music ushered in the Holy Spirit. It took me on a spiritual journey that called me closer to Him. I experienced a deeper meaning of sifting. It is where He is, and He will take us through everything. He is the Answer. He knows everything. I want and need to draw nigh unto Him. Through my afflictions, joys, and servanthood, I desire to be more like Him.

"Hear, O Israel: the LORD our God, the LORD is one."
(Deuteronomy 6:4, NIV)

The Master's Touch

"You show that you are a letter from Christ, the result of our ministry, written not with ink but with the Spirit of the of the living God, not on tablets of stone out on tablets of human hearts."
(2 Corinthians 3:3, NIV)

Still and waiting for someone to come,
A rose lays on the valley floor unscathed
By the torrential rains and the violent storms.
The harsh frost, the cold,
The terror in the darkness of the night,
The strong, scoffing wind chills
Each tender part of God's creation.
It is broken, but remains true and trusting
And faithful to its Creator.
Others have fallen around it,
Unable to withstand the peril.
Again it seeks rest,
And lays upon the valley floor,
The place where we are the closest to God.
A sound awakens it.
A rushing mighty wind,
The embrace of power,
Fills the air.
It is the Master,
And He cometh to rescue me!
The rose comes alive, and
Its sweet fragrance delights the Master.
It lifts high its head.
Its spirit is sweet with forgiveness,
Laced with redeeming grace,
And weaved with golden threads of hope.

The fragrance of Christ's divine love
Illuminates the world around it!
The rose has been kissed
By the heavenly dew,
Embraced by His holy presence,
Strengthened in its weakness,
And exalted by its endurance.
The rose looked up into
The Master's face and saw heaven.
It found a dwelling place in the nostrils of
The Holy Spirit's Divinity
Which drew it into His secret chamber –
The Throne Room.
An everlasting aroma
Lingers in His heart forever.

Can you identify yourself in this analogy? I can, with the things I've experienced over time. The Holy Spirit started revealing this to me when I was in my flower garden. My climbing rose was bitten by the harsh frost. There was one rose that laid on the ground, uninspired by the frost. Its stem was broken but not separated from the vine. I picked up the rose and put it back into the arbor. The cold frost and rain brought out its sweetness. I smelled the fragrance of that rose for a long time. It was the sweetest I had smelled all summer – God s Holy Presence creates a sweet aroma in our spirits.

Remnants of Grace Divine

The Cross –
A Divine sacrifice,
A Father's purposed will,
A Son's agonizing submission
To a dying and unsaved world.

Golgotha's Hill purified holy,
Cleansed with Mercy's blood,
Precious – Fragile – Sacred –
A Saviour's undying love.

Sin's unforgiving nails desiring to hold
An offering of sacrifice,
God's holy, unblemished Lamb,
Through love's piercing cold.

An Ecclesiastes garment,
Bloodstained threads of redemption,
Gambled by the ungodly hands
Of the soldiers,
Unaware of such unselfish love
And unbearable pain,
Soon to reap all their deeds done in vain.

The heavens passionately
Waited in silence
For God's will to be completed;
Soon the cross of death would be defeated.

Then the heavens opened up their arms
In angst splendor array,
With a loud trumpet reprise
Of darkness, thunder, and lightning,
Astonishing the unsuspecting crowd

Of onlookers that day.
This was not an ordinary scene,
Nor an ordinary man,
That died on Calvary's tree.

A soldier looked up and proclaimed,
"Truly this is the Son of God!"

Hallelujah – Hallelujah – Hallelujah

*"Praise the Lord for He has shown me
the wonder of His unfailing Love."
(Psalm 31:21)*

He Goes Before Me

"Do not be afraid or terrified of them, for the Lord your God goes before you, He will never leave you nor forsake you."
(Deuteronomy 31:8)

The inspiration for this writing came one night as I was walking home from our daughter's house. The moon was shining brightly over me, and cast a shadow before me. I knew God went before me, and His love assured me of His presence even in the darkness that surrounded me.

The luminous light of God's glory descended upon my shoulders as I walked into the darkness of the night. The shadows appeared before me, and I trembled, but I know He goes before me. He is my Shepherd, leading me. He is my Lamplight. I discern His Holy Presence. His light overpowers the darkness, and scatters it. I know the assurance of His love, and He promised to be with me always. For a season fear may come, and flow over my soul, but it will not possess me. It comforts me to know my Lord is by my side, walking with me.

God says I must keep my eyes focused on Him. I cannot stand still, however painful and uncertain it may be. I know He goes before me. He will establish my ways. He strengthens me so I can serve Him and accomplish His will. He goes with me, and together we will conquer.

Praising Him Forever

The Banquet Table

God's holy presence and His excellent glory:

The Setting – For His honored guests a table is reserved, graced in fine white linen, a symbol of purity.

Guests – the King of Glory and "His chosen," the Redeemed.

Atmosphere – Candles burning with sweet incense. We breathe into our whole inner being the sweet fragrance of His undying Love.

The Table – is spread before us with treasures of gold, silver, crystal, diamonds, and countless other gems. Symbols of His treasures given to "His chosen" from His Heart.

The Holy Wine – Coming from His Royal vineyard for a Royal priesthood. A sweet, sweet communion.

The Sanctified Bread – A sacrifice of Divine intervention for "His Holy Ones." A time to die to oneself. A purposeful calling to Christ. A promise to have no other gods before Him.

His Holy Reverence – illuminates the air. I behold Him as our spirits are baptized as one. I behold His eyes that are filled with compassion, mercy, and love. I am His destiny, His chosen one. A fulfillment, as one with Him, in Him, through Him. I've committed to walk in obedience, His will within Me. We make a solemn promise, a submissive will to serve together as one, the King and I.

"Come, for everything is now ready."
(Luke 14:17b, NIV)

Morning Glory

I marvel at such a loving,
Holy and merciful God!

Before me I behold the vision of
Your Holy Sanctuary,
Giving to me celestial images
Of royal amethyst,
Your aurora borealis
Of radiant brilliancy.

You consecrate my spirit and
Draw me into your Divine Deity.
O Son of Righteousness,
You are my Luminary.
You come forth as trillions
Upon trillions of glorious
Chandeliers that bring to me
Your grandeur and majesty.

With Your royal robe of
Righteousness you cover me, and
Seal your covenant in my heart.
Your royal flame purifies,
Releasing the luminous facets of
Heaven's holy lights.

Like arbors of Jehovah's
Eternal sweet flowers.
Royal hues of Your magnificent,
Immeasurable love is
Intertwined in the gardens
Of my heart.

I just love the purple morning glories, or any color of morning glories. Their colors enhance the world, and their vines are strong and unpredictable as to where they will go. How can a seed so tiny mature in such great dimensions? It is another one of God s miracles and mysteries, His creation of Grandeur and Glory.

For His Purpose and Glory

Seasons of Change

O Lord, how quickly the seasons change
As with the seasons in our own lives.

"I the LORD do not change ".
(Malachi 3:6a, NIV)

Even as now we enjoy the splendor of Your glory,
You have spread Your golden "garment of praise"
Through the hills of the countryside.

As another season awaits,
The earth comes to rest
In the silent beauty of a fresh fallen snow.
Quickly, the seasons seem to pass
With thoughts of spring on the wing,
When bluebirds will once again sing.

"Behold, I come quickly."
(Revelation 3:11a, KJV)

Other precious seasons have quickly gone
As each grandchild has grown into seasons of maturity.
They are the sweet spices in our lives,
Flavoring our lives rich with memories.

There are some things in our tomorrows
We are not always ready to face,
But will accept all things through
"His Presence always with us,"
His mending grace.

"'There is a time for everything,
and a season for every activity under heaven. "
("Ecclesiastes 3:1, NIV).

In the autumns of my life I seem to yearn even more for immortal blessings on my journey. Often God sends a storm cloud or two. Some are gilded in gold. These are special times shared just with my Lord. Through them He sets me upon eagle's wings, and renews my strength. (Isaiah 40:31).

It is awesome how the Holy Spirit gives us everything we need in our lives to exalt His worthy name, and to bring unto His courts, the honor and praise and glory due His Almighty name. As we were returning home one day we witnessed what seemed to be the clearing of storm clouds, but these were not ordinary. God had gilded them in gold. Our lives aren't ordinary. They are graced with His purpose. Before us were contrasts of His endless love and His all surpassing power, that left an indelible expression upon my spirit.

A Lamp Unto My Feet

Come and let us sit at the Master's feet. Can you see through His eyes into the eternal chamber of His heart? It is the main organ which carries His sacrificial blood of life to our veins, and His promise of everlasting life.

We do not walk alone. His presence is eternal, and amazingly wonderful. He never forgets us, forsakes us, or fails us. His love never fades. His love is deeper than the oceans, higher than the heavens, bigger than the earth, and it reaches down and lifts us up. He is our Hope, Refuge, Strength and Peace. It is abundant, boundless, beautiful, true, pure, priceless, wonderful, and awesome. He is the Holy Lamb of God, our Healer, the Anointed One, our Rose of Sharon, our Morning Star, our Eternal Friend, our Morning Glory, our Lily of the Valley, the Eastern Star, the Chosen One, the Light of Our World, our Provider, our Sustainer, our Deliverer, our Prophesied King, our Prince of Peace, the Faithful One, Emmanuel.

The name of Jesus melts away every obstacle, strengthens the weak, brings out the sun from behind a dark cloud, gives us peace in the midst of the storms and our valleys. He is Alpha and Omega, the Beginning and the End of all things.

Of all the books ever written, the Bible, chapter by chapter, stands the test of time. God is in control. His prophecies are right on time. Dear ones, take heart. Hang on through the rough places in your life, press through. God promises in His Word the Victory is ours. Hallelujah!

Praising Him Forever

The Face of Grace

I kissed the Holy Face of my Master;
Our spirits mingled as one.

I savored the sweetness of His awesome
Grace upon this Holy Face.

I felt His heart leap into mine.

His eyes envision my soul to create
In me more than I can be.

I ... perceived a sense of bitterness,
The gall of great sacrifice an
Awesome price to be paid ... at Calvary.

I saw ... within His Holy Face streams
Of mercy flowing down precious blood
Mingled with great compassion from
The thorns ... a twisted crown.

I bent to kiss His feet in our spirits.
Together we witnessed death He would defeat.

VICTORY ... WOULD BE WON – A TIME TO
CELEBRATE AS HE ESCAPED HELL ONLY
TO ENTER THROUGH HEAVEN'S GATE ... .

To Be As One

I am His princess,
And He is my beloved King.
I trust my life to Him:
He is my Everything.

His redeeming love is my everlasting covenant.
O King Divine,
I pledge to you my most valuable possessions,
My spirit and my soul,
As You my King
Had first given to me so long ago.

Your hands have fashioned me
A Heavenly Mansion,
And as I ascended there
It was far more beautiful than You ever shared.

It took my breath away!
Streets of gold,
Gates of pearl,
Walls of garnet, amethyst, and sapphire.
My soul delights within me
Because of who You are.

My Lord and my King – my Morning Star.

O my Lord, You know there is no other
Whom I have loved so deeply –
Your sacrifice, Your love for me
On Calvary.

Faithfully
I betroth my love to You,
My King Eternally

*Behold He comes! Can you see Him? O church, can
you see Him? He's coming for His bride, His church.
Prepare yourselves and get ready to meet Him in His
Royal Palace.   Now is the time to pledge your love to
the King of Glory.*

Mystery Wrapped in Love

O magnificently bright
And healing light,
The King's Shekinah glory,
A Divine Holy Presence,
A frame of mighty power,
A Father's embrace of unending love,
A life of righteousness and purity,
A plan of deliverance,
A Divine destiny.

Unblemished He came.
O Holy Lamb of God,
Innocent You remain.
O Divine One,
Who paid our price at the cross
In full,
A story written in blood,
Signed with redemption's love.

O Eternal Father who anoints
The holy pages
Down through time's endless ages,

Words of sword and of flame,

Proclaiming the Almighty power
In Jesus' name.

Unbearable the agony and suffering,
God's only Son,
Our destiny of an Eternal kingdom.

His Almighty love whispers
Of another world
Unmingled with sin,

Then God gives to us His
Living promise found in
The empty tomb.

Grief turns to joy!
Hallelujah!
He is Risen!

Our promise of Eternal Hope ...
Peace ... Life.
He has come to heal our broken hearts;
The Eternal Light
Has sacrificed
To cleanse us through His blood
Whiter than snow.
Oh, the soul – cleansing
Blood of the Lamb!

Hallelujah! What a Saviour!

Sometimes we just can't comprehend it all. A story too good to be true. But God made it possible, and He loves us this much. This is a mystery wrapped in God's unending love.

Love's Mystery

Serving Him

Love's Excelling Mystery

My precious Redeemer,
My sovereign Lord El' Elyon,
My Everlasting Saviour,
You become my Healer,
Jehovah Rapha,
Through those bloodstained
Garments of redemption.
You became my Righteousness from God,
Jehovah Tsidkenu.

Through Your discerning spirit
Came a holy fragrance of heaven's
Sweet perfume
Flowing from Your ivory palaces,
Jehovah Shammah.
O Divine Shekinah,
Adonai, Lord,
Alleluia!

Thou journeyed the path of sorrow
For my glory.
Mercy was by Your side.
Merciless Calvary.

'Twas love felt through Your
Bleeding, bruised feet.

Yea, not there alone, but through
Your God–Heart.

Jesus beheld a heavenly incense
As His Father's Holy Presence
Descended upon Him.

God felt each affliction His Son bore,
And held Him so very close from the throne,
For He, too, was the afflicted One.
He was vexed sore, and He wept;
In Holy Reverence He bowed down.
This was His only begotten Son
In whom He was well pleased,
For you see

He is flesh of His flesh,
Bone of His bone,
Spirit of His spirit.
Their blood sacrificed as one
To die for mortal man's sins
Oh, sweet love's excelling mystery!
He is love's excelling mystery.

And for those willing to follow
Him to steep Calvary,
They, too, shall receive
A Glorious Crown, A Royal Diadem!

Serving my EI Shaddai

*"To them God has chosen to make known among the
Gentiles the glorious riches of this mystery,
Which is Christ in you, the hope of glory."
(Colossians 1:27, NIV).*

My Precious Father

FATHER

I stand in awe of the cross...where
You gave for me...Your all.

Release the splendor of your Glory;
Bear me above where streams flow
Of Your mercy and of Your love.

Sustain me in Your inner being,
In the secret chamber...of Your heart.

Create in...me not ways of mine, but
The giving...of myself wholly to Thine.

Precious Father...come and
Meet...me where I am.

Carry me...away into Your arms.

Hold me...like one of Your lambs.

Tenderly...with Your heart of compassion,
Say to me...I am all thine own, and gently
Guide my footsteps to my eternal destiny.

In the Shadow of His Grace

Even in the shadows I...will not fear
For I...can feel His Holy Presence
Yes...He is very near

Even in my times of doubt He is there to bring
Me from under and out in my times of no understanding.
He is there...standing by me

IN THE SHADOW OF HIS GRACE.

IN EARTH'S SHADOW

HE IS HEAVEN'S HOLY LIGHT

When the pain of confusion overwhelms He is
With me...even still in His arms He carries...me
Oh...so very well
When I grope in the darkness, and the way
Seems to overcome, I know my faith in God
Will carry me through, and hope will succumb
I know I am His child

I AM MORE THAN A CONQUEROR THROUGH HIM

He is my Beacon in the night
I shall stand...victoriously

IN THE GLORY...OF HIS...HOLY LIGHT

"You have made known to me the path of life."
(Psalm 16:11a, NIV)

Glory to the Lamb

GLORY TO THE LAMB OF GOD

GLORY TO THE LAMB

I stand amazed of my Jesus the Crucified and wonder how He
Could love...me a sinner condemned to die

GLORY TO THE LAMB OF GOD

GLORY TO THE LAMB

How could He walk that lonely hill to Calvary
How did He bear that cruel cross for...me...?

GLORY TO THE LAMB OF GOD

GLORY TO THE LAMB

To the cross...Himself...He gave
For me...a sacrifice...His **amazing grace**

GLORY TO THE LAMB OF GOD

GLORY TO THE LAMB

He shed His Blood...preciously...over the cross He reigns
My soul will forever sing

GLORY TO THE LAMB OF GOD

GLORY TO THE LAMB

Wellspring of His Righteousness

Precious Father, I ... come to Thee: fill ... me
With Your Holiness - Your Victory.

Lift me up to heaven's throne;
Take my spirit ... into Your own,
Into Your ethereal Glory.

Precious ... Lord,
Of You I want even more.

I yearn to feel my spirit soar
Freely from this earthly shore.

I cannot explain as I "whisper" Your Holy Name.

I cannot fathom Your mighty pow'r
Nor know how awesome and hallow'd.

Nor do I know how Divine
'Til You hold my hand in Thine.

How can I say I know You
Until I've walked by your side?

How can I say I love You
Until I stand ... in awe of the cross crucified

How can I say naught of Thee
'Til by Your merciful grace You have cleansed me ...?

Face to Face
(With God)

I feel Your Holy Presence
Go ... before me.

I see your passing
From the leaves
On the trees

I "whisper" the holy name of "Jesus"
In my spirit I know ... You are very near

From heaven's holy sphere
You ... are
The holy fragrance ... the incense of desire

Your love is as awesome and beautiful
As ... heaven;
You betroth me to come unto Your Divine Spirit

Your promises woo me to
Become Thine own

Let the temple of Your Spirit flow free
I am as one ... but betrothed ... as to Three

Oh ... Holy Lamb of God,
Thou preparest a wedding feast
Where my soul can come and dine

Adorned in fine white linen
We sanctify this sweet communion

On this our Holy Day
Together ... we celebrate

The ... King and I ... .
(Isaiah 55:11, 12)

Ecclesiastes of a Divine Teacher

A BASIN OF LIVING WATER

An anointed cleansing ... pure from sin,
Jesus ... our Divine Teacher,
Jesus' disciples ... and you and I,
A muttering of understanding,
But ... with a Divine purpose.

A BASIN OF LIVING WATER

A holy garment destined to be stained,
A sacred sacrifice to sanctify.

A BASIN OF LIVING WATER

The time of God's anointing,
A time for Jesus ... a reflection
On what will yet be
A time of preparation
For those appointed to ponder
For soon ... on Calvary's hill
This moment will become real,
For the precious Lamb of God
Has sacrificed His life-giving blood
For all ... a ransom to receive.

THIS DIVINE TEACHER ... TO BELIEVE ... .

O, Magnify the Name of Our Lord

All the earth
Magnify the name of our Lord.
His throne is set in higher places;
There are treasures that
Have not been revealed.

The treasures of His mighty works,
The hand of our Almighty God.

I glorify You, O, Holy One;
I lift my spirit up to You
To be fulfilled.

O, magnify the name of our Lord!

O, Master Divine,
Humble my spirit 'til I see
Only...Thine.

The angels sing in Your midst.

Great is Jehovah.

All praise and glory belong to Thee,
O, Blessed Lamb of Calvary.
Praise to the unblemished Lamb.
With Your unselfish sacrifice
Of Your precious blood
You freed me.
I am cleansed,
Yes...cleansed indeed.

O, magnify the name of our Lord!
All praise and all glory to the Lamb.
How can I ever repay,
Of the calling You have
Given to me.

O, magnify the name of our Lord!

Simply Because He Loves You

Jesus ... God's only begotten Son
Was scorned, rejected, and abused
He gave up His life ... a ransom for all

He was accused,
But never convicted.

The crown of thorns
Pierced
His precious head,
Simply because He loves you

He willingly carried "my" cross
Up Calvary's hill
Each step He took for me
Unselfishly,
His weary feet bleeding and bruised
Against the jagged rock,
Simply because He loves you

He died blameless
Simply because He loves you
He was laid inside a garden tomb,
This unblemished Lamb of God
A perfect sacrifice was He

The time has come
For His Father to say,
"Son ... come ... home."
He allowed Him to die in my place.
Oh, unutterable mercy and grace,
Oh, how He missed Him so!

In "my" place ... He loved "me" enough to go.
Jesus, our Saviour ... God's beloved Son
Conquered death ... Victory is won.

There is born a glorious new dawn
A new life we can begin –
At the tomb Jesus freed us from our sin.
Glory ... hallelujah!
Glory to the Lamb!
All praise and honor
To this Blessed One,
God's resurrected Son.

Sifted Through His Hands

In my times of weakness
He sifts me through to
The power of His strength.

Whenever the thorns prick my soul,
And they cause me great pain,
I know 'twas given to me
For heaven's gain.

I know I must press on,
For God has a plan in place
Through His miracle grace.

O thorn of pain,
My richest gain
Is heaven's bright morning.
His Shekinah Glory I shall see,
For by His thorn, He strengthened me.

*"Because of the surpassing greatness of the revelations,
for this reason, to keep me from exalting myself,
there was given me a thorn in the flesh, a messenger of Satan
to torment me—to keep me from exalting myself!"
(2 Corinthians 12: 7, NASB).*

*"The LORD is my light and my salvation; whom shall I fear?
The LORD is the strength of my life; of whom shall I be
afraid?"
(Psalm 27: 1, KJV).*

Sunset Over the Mountain

In glorious expectations,
Surrounded by God's throne
Of holy light,
Just beyond the glowing amber
And the organdy lavender hue,
Our Saviour has built
A mansion there
For me and you.

I see, O radiant splendor;
I marvel at your turquoise veil.
I praise You, Precious Lord.
Your love for me has never failed.

O ecstasy of celestial light,
O torch of flaming red,
Soon we will meet face to face.
By Your nail-scarred hands I am led.

I will soar heaven's heights;
By Your scarred side I will stand
In the mansion beyond the sunset,
O Shekinah land!

*While vacationing in Arizona we were returning home
late one evening when God ended a perfect day with
this outstanding sunset cresting the mountain.*

*"... And causes the light of His cloud to shine?"
(Job 3 7:15, NKJV)*

Holy Oil of Healing

I am a vessel of clay.
Prepare me
To receive
Your sweet fragrant oil of incense.

Flow into my inner chamber
Your Holy Presence;
O glorious flame,
Trim the wick of my soul.
Let me be only honor and praise
To Your Holy Name,
A holy glow.

Fill this vessel
With Your living fountain of oil;
Transform my will to be
The sweet, fragrant oil of Your Spirit,
Aglow with the light of brilliance,
Your eternal luminescence.

It is well with my soul
That Your nail-pierced hands of Calvary
Trim away the black, charred wick of self,
To gleam within my soul
Your purifying grace.
I come as a vessel
Ready to be
A light glowing radiantly
FOR THEE ... .

"Aaron shall burn on it sweet incense every morning;
when he tends the lamps ..."
(Exodus 30:7, NKJV).
Exodus 37:25·28 describes the "altar of incense."

"You are the light of the world ..."
(Matthew 5:14-16, NIV)

114

With Feet of Clay

With feet of clay
I am not worthy
To walk proclaiming
Your awesome name,

But through Your sacrifice
On a cross ... for a King
Worthy I became.

I may not have my name
In the world's famous book,
But it's in the "Lamb's Book of Life."
There's so much more to gain
Than worldwide fame.

I may not live in a fancy home,
But someday I'll live in
A palace of gold.

I don't walk in darkness,
But in God's Holy Glow.
I don't walk on a rocky path,
But up the King's heavenly road.

I possess no wealth,
But Jesus lives in my heart.
His riches out measure
All this world's treasures.

*"Hath not the potter power over the clay, of the same
lump to make - one vessel unto honour, and another
unto dishonour?"*
(Romans 9:21, KJV).

Silently Falls His Majestic Name

How silently...God's love falls
Upon the earth,
Like the wondrous beauty
Of a soft fallen snow,
The blanket of His magnificent love.

From heaven God's exquisite beauty
Is proclaimed;
Like His awesome power from on high,
Silently falls His majestic name.
Silently...a radiant light appears,
Our gift from heaven.
On a blessed morn
A sweet baby Boy...
Our Saviour...was born.

Silently...Mary the mother of Jesus
Wraps her sweet Baby in a garment
Of tender love.

Soon a Garment of Sacrifice will be given.
A Holy Garment with the radiance of God's love
Will be the eternal glory of heaven,
His Shekinah glory,
The bright light that will shine
In full array,
A Glorified Garment of Praise
For all of God's sanctified.
Will proclaim
His majestic name!!

"Bless the Lord, O my soul!
O Lord my God, You are very great:
You are clothed with honor and majesty,
Who cover Yourself with light as with a garment...."
(Psalm 104:1-4, NKJV)

116

The Only Begotten

Jesus suffered at Calvary
For ... me.
He became "my" sacrifice,
And carried "my" cross
Upon His wounded back.

HE BECAME THE SACRIFICIAL LAMB OF GOD.

He felt the blow of the hammer
Tear through His hands and His feet;
His pain He bore was for "me."
The sword that thrusts His side
Opened a river that flowed from
Calvary's tide,
For His precious blood
Cleansed me.
My soul rejoices, "I am redeemed!"

ALLELUIA!

Down from the cross Jesus came;
From the tomb of the night
He became God's resurrected Light.

God, Our Father,
HAS EXALTED HIS
Only begotten Son.
HIS NAME IS JESUS,
THE CHOSEN ONE.

"I have come as a light into the world that whoever
abides in Me should not abide in darkness."
(John 12:46, NKJV)

A Land Beyond Time

You left me for a land beyond time,
A land for eternity,
A place where we will be together someday,
You and me.

A place where God our Father
Reigns with all the glory of His presence,
A land where we will feel no more sorrow,
Where yesterday hands forth no tomorrows:
There's just eternity.

On the mountain top we will always be,
And the flowers will bloom everlastingly,
Where the river of God runs free.

You walked from earth to heaven,
A journey through time;
The Father held your hand
On the way up to Glory.
Someday I, too, will follow,
But for now ... He holds mine ... .

*"...I am the light of the world. He who follows Me
shall not walk in darkness, but have the light of life."
(John 8:12, NKJV)*

*In Memory of Don Krigbaum, my dear Brother in
Christ, January 2010, and my dear Sister in Christ
(his wife) Kitty, October 2010*

Just a Ray of Sun

Just a ray of sun
Upon this dreary day,
Just a feeling of warmth
Wrapped around me when I pray,
Just a tear of understanding
In a struggling time,
Just a touch of your hand onto mine,
Just a simple smile
Upon a weary face,
Just a promise of caring
In this special moment of sharing.

Just a little bit of time,
And some everyday small talk,
Just someone on this journey
That together with me will walk.

Just someone with me,
A friend, the Lord and I,
Just someone before I must meet
My Lord in the sky,
Someone to care,
Yes, just someone to be there.

> *"... Even the night shall be light about me."*
> *(Psalm* 139:9-11, *NKJV)*

The elderly carry a special place in my heart. They yearn for attention, and oh, the rewards we glean by giving them just a little of ourselves.

An Angel With a Broken Wing

I walk with you through the
Sunshine and rain
Over the bridge of your troubled soul.

From the deep shadows of your life
God calls tenderly,
"Come ... and ... follow ... Me."

Even in the deserts you
Struggle to survive.
I will give to you
"My ... Living Water,"
A bountiful and awesome supply,
A wellspring that will never run dry.

You are always in a hurried lifestyle.
I am there ... I caution you at the
Stoplights of your heart.
I want you to stop for a while,
And listen ... listen ... for, with a still,
Small voice,
God ... your Creator will speak
Of His Healing Peace.

God has sent me to watch over you
As a father ... He watches ... tenderly.
Sometimes you do childish things,
And you stumble ... with your heart broken.
I will ... be there ... to pick you up
Again ... and ... again.
The pieces of your heart
God ... tearfully mends,
Compassionately,
At the end of your trying day.

Finally ... you sit ... quietly.
Restless sleep will only come
While this angel weeps,
For God's presence again this day
You chose not to seek.

Often, God speaks to me in the simple circumstances of our lives. When a storm came through our area, our concrete angel fell from its pedestal, and broke the tip of a wing. A confirmation came to the writing of this poem when I attended our parish seminar on prayer at the Main Street United Methodist Church in New Albany, Indiana in August of 1998.

"Commit your way to the Lord, trust also in Him, and He shall bring it to pass. He shall bring forth your righteousness as the light... ."
(Psalm 37:5, 6, NKJV)

"... Lo, I am with you always, even unto the end of the world. Amen."
(Matthew 28:20, KJV)

Master! The Tempest Is Raging

Master ... the tempest is raging in my soul,
And the waves are so steep.
My dear child ... I am with you;
In My hands your soul I will keep.

Master ... I hear the mighty thunder roll.
My precious child ... I am with you there.
Do not be afraid ... it is I;
I have everything in control.

Master ... I hear the strong winds of adversity blow.
Yes, My sweet child ... I am with you.
Do not be afraid:
Peace ... Be ... Still.
The calmness shall fill your soul.

The sail of this ship is battered.
Yes, I know, Lord, You are with me even here.
In Your voice of sweet assurance
You gather together "my" battle.

Master ... with Your hands of Calvary
You mend these, Your storm-tattered sails,
And you say to me, "My child, thee I will not fail.
Behold! You shall conquer the storm
Through My power I have given to thee."

I'll stay close by your side
And guide the compass of your heart
Where I will eternally abide."

*"When you pass through the waters, I will be with
you; Fear not, for I am with you ... ."
(Isaiah 43:2-5, NKJV)*

*I send poetry through my card ministry, but this
certain day the Holy Spirit beckoned me to go and
read this poem to a friend. Through this she thanked
me, and God brought her peace and took her home to
be with Him.*

Oasis in the Desert

O Living Water, flow
Through my soul,
And refresh my spirit.

O Blessed Rock of Ages,
Thou hast planted my feet
On Your solid rock.

O Shepherd of the Hills,
Thou shall provide
Refreshing streams
In the dry lands.
All things Thou suppliest
By Thine own blessed hands.

Thou shalt surround me with Your
Enchanted realm of love,
Your awesome Spirit
From my heavenly home above.

I've felt the holy sweetness
Of Your touch
Fall upon me,
Your Holy Spirit running free.

As the streams flow of Your mercy,
Captivating my soul,
For You are the brook that flows
Within me,
With eternal power

Generating Your love,
Fulfilling Your plan,
Your glory is brought forth through me.
To Thee be all honor, praise and
GLORY.

*"As the hart panteth after the water brooks, so
panteth my soul after thee, O God. My soul thirsteth
for God, for the living God .... "*
(Psalm 42:1-2, KJV)

By His Hand

O darkened pathway
I know I must tread,
Sorrow is woven in it,
But still by Your hand
I am led.

You cast forth a shadow
From Your mighty hand
To fulfill in me
Your Divine plan.
I do not know where the
Pathway leads,
But I trust in You, and I believe.

I know I must withstand
The sorrow and the pain,
For through them
Your secret treasures
Will be revealed and retained.

No more the pathway of sorrow,
For now the darkness leads to light
As it passes through
The shades of the night,
For my God in love
Has unveiled the way.
I rest in His unchanging grace.

"... He knows what is in the darkness,
And the light dwells with Him."
(Daniel 2:22, NASB)

The Sunroom (God's Throne)

The sunroom is God's throne.
Oh, the Shekinah glory that is
Present there;
O celestial light that warms
My soul;
I've come to praise You,
O Holy One.
I've come to bask in Your awesome glow.

Shower me with Your Holy Rain,
As in the refreshment of a babbling stream
That flows through the desert,
For You O Lord watereth my soul

From the fresh springs of
Your Living Water.
An anointing of joy overflows
As it gracefully falls upon me;
It is like rainbows of spray from
Your eternal fountain,
Cleansing and making me whole.

OUR SPIRITS EMBRACE ONE ANOTHER.

O overwhelming glory,
O communion so wonderfully sweet!
My soul is bathed in Your awesome glory
While sitting at my King's feet.
O holy fragrance,
Surround ... me
With Your Divine majesty.

O HOLY ONE,
I praise You for the sunroom
Of Your glorious throne,
And the fresh anointing of Your glory.

I came, O King of Glory,
And behold! You freely gave!
You filled this vessel of clay
Up to overflowing.

> *"...God is light and in Him is no darkness at all."*
> *(1 John 1:5, NKJV)*

In a rehab center in Corydon, Indiana, there is a beautiful sunroom with plants and flowers growing there. The Holy Spirit drew me to the warm and glowing Light. The Shekinah Glory of God shines there, and it is through this that the title and thoughts of this poem came into existence. This is a great place for ministry. I go there on occasion and visit with the patients, especially one elderly gentleman who loves company, but they all have a hunger for a few moments of our time.

"There shall be no night there: They need no lamp nor light of the sun, for the Lord God gives them light ... ."
(Revelation 22:5, NKJV)

Tears of Release

Tears of release:
Oh, how I cried!
Then ... I felt the deep release
Come deep inside –
It released ... and gave to me
Such awesome peace!

I knew Jesus was right there,
Right where I am;
He came and released these tears.
He is the Great I Am.

How can I tell of the sweetness
That came to my soul?
For through those tears He cleansed
Me and made me whole!
Through this pain
I overcame,
For through it all
He sustains.

I cannot explain
What transforms
When Jesus comes,
But this I know:
In His voice of blessed assurance,
Through His amazing grace,
He so wondrously restores.

"Oh, send out Your light and Your truth! Let them lead me; let them bring me to Your holy hill and to Your tabernacle."
(Psalm 43:3, NKJV)

His Awesome Glory

Glory ... such awesome Glory!

Let Thy radiance come ... and
Fall upon me.

I hear heaven's angels singing
In harmonious jubilee.

Far ... far ... beyond
The clouds of pearl

A mansion is waiting.
Jesus is beckoning me to come,
Escaping this sinful world.

Peace will surround Him,
Love will rule His kingdom.

Faith and hope we need no more,
For we left them behind when
We entered through heaven's door.

I know I can never comprehend,
But someday I shall know it;
His glory will never end ... .

*When we exercise our spiritual gifts, it is as if Christ
Himself reaches down to take care of one of His own.*

Heaven – How Majestic!

Yes, even on a very trying day when I felt much unrest in my spirit, God came so awesomely close to me. He gives to me a wellspring of His assurance. I would not be able to begin to write anything without the steadfast guidance of the Holy Spirit. The pen is always flowing with His wellspring that will never run dry. His "scrolls of love" continue ... .

Oh ... Great Shepherd, come to me and guide me, for my directions seem blurred ... the storms are getting more violent now, and the rains of fear and doubt are upon me. I pray for Yehshua's staff to pull me to safety. Deliver me from my enemies. Thy rod and Thy staff, they comfort me in my times of uncertainty. You are my great Shepherd who holds me like a lamb in Your arms. Anchor me in the bosom of Your heart where Your love surrounds me and understands my soul that dwells inside of You. You are the Spirit that lives within me, that is awesome and overwhelming, yet ... with majestic power that overcomes me and consumes my soul and surrounds me into the realm of Your glory ... Your holy presence of timeless praise ... yes, I greet You in the name of our blessed Father Yahweh and the Shepherd of the Hills, Yehshua. There is none who holds me in his arms and hears the beatings of my heart like You do.

HEAVEN ... HOW MAJESTIC IS YOUR NAME!!!!!

Step out and go with God. He will meet you, not at the end of the road, not in the middle, but with your first step.

Prism of His Love

A rainbow of crystalline,
A sacred song of light,
Awesome splendor of His presence.

A prophesy of brilliance,
His robe flowing,
Transparent ... iridescent,
His face glowing
As a Crystal Prism:
Catch a gleam of His Divine Holiness.

His majestic name is proclaimed;
Glory ... His shekinah ... Glory.
Carry forth the Royal Diadem;
Encircle Him with garlands of praise.

Bring forth the garment of redemption,
A ransom paid in full for all our sin;
CROWN ... HIM ... CROWN ... HIM.
We have been ... redeemed;
We ... are ... set free.

GLORY ... GLORY
TO THE KING ... OF KINGS!
Lift your hands ... in praise of
Honor and Royalty.

HE ... IS ... THE LORD OF LORDS,
THE GREAT ... I AM,
THE UNBLEMISHED LAMB!
ALLELUIA ... ALLELUIA!
CROWN HIM ... CROWN HIM
LORD OF ALL,
LORD OF ALL.

Iridescence: A display of gleaming and shimmering colors. Giving a display of colors like those of a rainbow.

Prism (Priz' um): Glass or other transparent substance that decomposes light into its spectrum ... reflections of light.

"And he that sat was to look upon like a jasper and a sardine stone: and there was a rainbow round about the throne, in sight like unto an emerald."
(Revelation 4:3, KJV)

The Master Builder

JESUS ... OUR ... ROCK ... OF ... AGES

We build our extravagant homes,
And we possess acres of land,
But still ... we are only ... man.
God is God,
And He is the Divine Creator over all.

He owns the cattle on a thousand hills,
And ... He ... has a master plan in each
Of our lives to be fulfilled.

JESUS ... OUR ... ROCK ... OF ... AGES

He sacrificed His heavenly domain
For our souls to reclaim.
Those earthly possessions will
Someday be left behind,
For a mansion is being built
By the hands of the "One Divine."

It will not be constructed of
Earthly materials
Of rock, wood, and of nails.

No earthquakes or floods or winds
Will destroy.

This mansion's structure will be
Exceedingly precious jewels,
And its foundation will never fail.

JESUS ... OUR ... ROCK ... OF ... AGES

We come broken ... to be restored
By the Master's hand;

With each splinter of pain
We labor to persevere.
Our heavenly treasures will not perish
As they will ... on this earthly sphere.

We are carved into His image,
Designed for eternity.

The Architect has drawn His final plan;
The essence of His glory
Will someday be mine
When this earthly temple is left behind.

JESUS ... OUR ... ROCK ... OF ... AGES

A Majestic Morning Glory

In the cool of the morning
I was led to go into my garden

Where a royal purple morning glory
Has inherited the world.
Its breathtaking beauty
Overwhelms me,
As I ponder the deep things of our Lord.

"I am the Vine ... ye are the branches";
He beckons me to come and dine
Into the vineyard of royal wine.

They clothed You in purple
Upon the golden altar;
You became an anointed Sacrifice,
You became a Lamp of light,
To carry Your people through the night.

Lift this veil of self
From this Your temple;
Cleanse me with Calvary's blood:

I am an heir to Your royal Priesthood.
May I never forget
That You are my King.

MY MAJESTIC MORNING GLORY

"Coming to Him as to a living stone, rejected indeed by men, but chosen by God and precious, you also, as living stones, are being built up a spiritual house, a holy priesthood, to offer up spiritual sacrifices acceptable to God through Jesus Christ."
(1 Peter 2:4, 5, NKJV)

An Image of You

One day ... I prayed,
"Lord ... make me more like You."
The valley I walked through ...
Became so dark ... but I was not alone.

Not realizing the full intent,
The price of full sacrament ...
An image of ... You ... Father,
I stand in awe

As you teach me
The deep things ... of God ... .

In Your hand You hold the anvil,
And then ... the spike;
You begin to teach me
What it means to sacrifice ... .

I cried, "No, Lord ... please ... I didn't mean ... .
Why must it be so painful?"
"Child ... I have a plan
And a purpose for you;
Together ... we must carry it through ... .
Like Me ... you wanted to be;

"You must humble yourself, and nail
To the cross your earthly desires.
You are the one ... I have chosen
To show others My love.

"Your sacrifice ... will be our gain,
For ... through ... you ... I ... will ... lift ... up
My Almighty Name ... .
It is by the sacrificial wounds
Of your heart
That you will be healed ... . "

Oh ... Jerusalem

Oh ... how far have you wandered
From Me!
I am no longer your Pilot by day,
Or your Shepherd ... when falls the night.
Oh ... Jerusalem.

Your ears are no longer open;
Your heart has turned away.
No longer do you recognize me as your God;
Your eyes have become blinded;
Your heart is as hard as the stone.

Your faith is gone ... it has flown away
On the wings of the dove.
Oh ... Jerusalem ... how far will you go!
You have left Me for another love,
A love you have idolized all your own.

Out on the hillsides ... My flocks
Have no shepherd.
Oh ... precious lambs ... I Am That I Am;
I am calling ... to thee
While you are lost and bleating ... .
I am your Saviour ... come ... follow Me;
I will lead you across the barren land
Into a country flourishing with manna.
Come ... follow ... Me ...
And I will sustain thee ... .
Oh ... Jerusalem ... I love you!

A **Faithful Servant**

My Lord ... my Saviour,
Don't ever stop loving me;
Teach me to be faithful.

Fill my heart ... again ... with Your praise;
Come and sit near me ... please stay ...
Until I am relieved of this pain.

My Lord ... I long to be with You;
I don't want to face these tomorrows
With these new sorrows.

If I could hear the birds sing
Their sweet song in the day,
Their harmonious praise ... .

It's been so long since I've had
Content and sweet rest;
Sin beckons at my heart's door
To come and molest ...
My painful heart.

My Lord ... my Saviour,
Interlace my heart with Yours,
And restore ... .
Take away this pain;
Let me just ... rest here
Beside this babbling stream ... .

We become stronger in the Lord when we are the weakest.

Show Me Thy Ways

Yahweh ... I greet you
This blessed morn
While the day is as
Fresh as the dew.

I look up into the hills;
I feel the wonderful presence of You
Giving to me Your Divine
Strength for another day.

Show me Thy ways,
O Precious One;
Guide me along Your familiar
Pathways when I feel alone.

I know You are my Great Shepherd
That will keep me by Your side;
Whether in weakness or in strength,
In you I will eternally abide .

(Psalm 121)

While doing missions in California in 1997, Janet and Kathy and I took a refreshing mornings walk. Kathy lived in the valley. I experienced a sweet presence of my Lord that morning.

From This Day Forward

From this day forward I will
Be a new creation.
I will reach far and beyond;
I will reach for hope,
And find it there.

I will reach beyond despair ... .
Take my hand and lead me on
To the Glory of Thy celestial sun.

I looked up and beheld this wondrous light,
For God has made a way for me
Through the darkness of the night ... .

I will reach out for faith,
For I believe all things are
Possible through Him.

My hope is a candle with an eternal flame,
For when I reached out Jesus reached in ...
And healing came.

From this day forward
I will reach beyond ...
The glory of the majestic dawn.

"Have you ever given orders to the morning,
or shown the dawn its place?"
(Job 38:12, NIV)

At Crest of Hill

I expect to see at crest of hill
The glories of God.
When I thought I could stand ... I fell;
With His loving arms He lifted me.
When I thought I was strong ... I was weak;
It was then God gave to me His strength.
When I thought there was darkness,
There was this "Glorious Light."
Strong winds – fierce their mighty gale,
But I know my Lord will never fail.
When I thought the end must be near,
It was only the beginning:
I must endure ... I must persevere.
When I walk through the fire,
It is then I will be made stronger.
I am just a lump of clay being molded
By the gentle hands of the Potter ... .

Do we find the Lord shaping us? I have a lot of rough edges to be chiseled and polished by the Master. It's painful, but the process makes us stronger in doing the work He calls us to do. As He lovingly chisels, He molds us into His Likeness, the image of His Soul. Amen.

Empty of Tears
(Mary, the Mother of Jesus)

Empty of tears,
A heart ripped apart,
A void felt beyond repair.
My heart feels empty and dark
As I kneel beneath this cross.

Our precious Son, Jesus:
How can they nail this innocent
Man, our only Son,
To a cruel, rugged cross?
How can they mock and ridicule
Our Son who has done no wrong?
An angry mob,
What have they become?

My poor heart aches with pain
As we take from the cross our Son Slain ... .

We wrapped him, our beloved Son,
In the finest white linen,
And laid Him in a cold stone grave.
Then they rolled the stone
That sealed Him away ... .

THEN BEHOLD!!
THE STONE WAS ROLLED AWAY.
HALLELUJAH! !
DARKNESS OF NIGHT
TURNED INTO DAY.
OUR SON NOW LIVES A RESURRECTED KING.
GLORY TO HIS NAME!!
MY HEART LEAPS IN JOYOUS REFRAIN,
FOR OUR SON LIVETH AGAIN ...
HALLELUJAH!! HALLELUJAH!!

In the Secret of His Presence

I know my Redeemer liveth,
And the sun shall rise
On tomorrow.
But then, if not,
I know I shall meet Him
In the Eastern sky.
Blessed Assurance!

The raindrops
Need the sun
To bud a flower,
And so it is with the
Secret Presence of God,
To know His magnificent Power.

The sound of rain fell
Peacefully against my window,
Showering me with blessings,
And comforting me with
His warm Embrace.

In the secret of His Presence
How my soul delights to hide,
As I learn precious lessons
From my Saviour's side

When my soul is faint and thirsty
'Neath the shadow of His Wing,
There is a cool and pleasant shelter,
And a fresh and crystal spring.

To know the sweetness of
The secret of the Lord,
Go and hide beneath His Shadow:
This shall be thy sweet reward.

And whenever you leave the silence
Of that Happy Meeting Place,
Your mind will bear the image
Of the Master on your face.

My deepest joy and desire is to be in the secret place. Silence is a beautiful thing in this fast-paced world. It freely gives me strength and hope and peace each new morning. Some stanzas of this poem were selected from a 153-year-old sacred hymn book given to me by a precious friend on the eve of two years ago. God meant for His treasures to be cherished and shared by others! My friend's life was almost taken from her. God is always ahead of any evil game meant to destroy. "... Ye thought evil against me; but God meant it unto good, to bring to pass, as it is this day ..." (Genesis 50:20, KJV). This verse is one of the greatest promises of God. He can take the evil which is planned against the believer – that is, if the believer fully trusts – and turn it to good, until there is nothing left but good.

"He who dwells in the shelter of the Most High will abide in the shadow of the Almighty. I will say to the LORD, My refuge and my fortress, my God, in whom I trust!" (Psalm 91:1-2, NASB)

It is no secret what God can do –

Above the Clouds

Far above the clouds of white,
Someday I will take my eternal flight;
With an escort of angels from on high
I will bid this world goodbye ... .

Loved ones will meet me at heaven's gate;
Through all of life's trials
It will be worth the wait ... .

I marvel at all of heaven's treasure,
Far more beauty than my mind could measure.

Jewels more brilliant than a rainbow's glare,
And golden streets to walk on there ...
An angel's wings spread in full array,
Singing with joy on that blessed day ... .

But more than anything I want to see
Christ my Lord who died for me ... .
I see Him seated on glory's throne
As He takes my hand and leads me home ... .

Far above the clouds of white
Someday I will take my heavenly flight;
With an escort of angels from on high
I will bid this world goodbye.

*Janet Rae and I wrote this poem together on our flight
to California to do missions in 1997.*

The Winds of His Spirit

Lord ... I see You so awesomely
Standing before me;
In Your presence I feel I must
Reach out and touch ...
Your glory with my soul.

Let obedient hands be raised
In reverential praise ... .
Let Yahshua's name be exalted
At heaven's altar.

I see Your garment flowing free,
Your Spirit flowing through me.

I cannot look upon Your face;
I can only feel Your overwhelming embrace ... .
I see a vision .... When I contain the whole,
It will be glory for my soul ... .

I Am That I Am

I Am more than
A porcelain figurine;
I Am more than
A beautiful stained glass window.

I Am more, for I Am supreme.

I Am eternal ... I Am
The First and the Last.
I Am the Lord of lords
And the King of kings;
I Am He who holds the keys ...
To heaven and hell.
Behold! I Am He that liveth.

I Am the Living Sacrifice
For your sins.
I Am of a higher court ...
I Am your Supreme Judge;

I Am the Almighty Power
In this universe.
I Am He that will return someday
To receive you unto myself.

I AM THAT I AM

*"I am he that liveth, and was dead; and behold, I am
alive for evermore, Amen; and have the keys of life
and of death."*
(Revelation 1:18, KJV)

Pressing Through with Encouragement

Rewards of Righteousness: (2 *Timothy* 1:9) Allowing Christ to fulfill His purpose in their lives, they were conformed to His image *(Romans 8:29)* in every area of their lives.

The Watcher's Crown: The meritorious award will be given to all who watch for Christ's return. *(II Timothy 4:8) "Henceforth there is laid up for me a crown of righteousness which the Lord, the Righteous Judge, shall give me at that day; and not to me only, but unto all them also that love His appearing."*

The Runner's Crown: The reward found in *I Corinthians 9:24-27, "Know ye not that they which run in a race run all, but one receiveth the prize? So run, that ye may obtain. And every man that striveth for the mastery is temperate in all things. Now they do it to obtain a corruptible crown; but we an incorruptible. I therefore so run, not as uncertainly; so fight I, not as one that beateth the air; but I keep under my body, and bring it into subjection; lest that by any means, when I have preached to others, I myself should be a castaway."*

The Shepherd's Crown: *(1 Peter 5:1-4) Faithful Ministers Reward. "The elders which are among you I exhort, who am also an elder, and a witness of the sufferings of Christ, and also a partaker of the glory that shall be revealed; Feed the flock of God which is among you...."*

(please read the entirety of this scripture passage.)

The Soul Winner's Crown: Awarded to soul winners. *(Daniel 12:3) "And they that be wise shall shine as the brightness of the firmament; and they that turn many to righteousness as the stars forever and ever."*

The Sufferer's Crown: *(James 1:12) "Blessed is the man that endureth temptations (testing and trial); for when he is tried, he shall receive the crown of life, which the Lord has promised to them that love Him." (Also, read Matthew 5:10-12)*

Matthew 25:21: *"Well done thou good and faithful servant."*

Galatians 6:9 *"And let us not be weary in well doing for in due season we shall reap, if we faint not. "*

Royalty Upon a Hill

Royalty was crucified upon Calvary's hill;
There Jesus' precious blood was spilled ...
Upon that old rugged cross
For you and for me.
He died there for all eternity

A crown of thorns was placed
Upon His precious head
Where there should have been
A Royal Crown instead.

His earthly raiment about His
Frail and weakened body
Should have been His Royal Robe.

The spikes that held His
Innocent hands and feet
Was a plan between Father and Son
Our destiny to complete.

He cried, "It is finished," that day.

How can we repay,
But kneel before the King of kings
As a servant called out
To gain a royal home ... .

Jesus left His last "will and testament, "He died ... yet
He arose in Victory. He came back from the grave to
see that "whosoever will" would receive all His Riches
in Glory ... .

Ribbon of Love

Lord ... I come to Thee.
You have promised to fill my cup:
I come believing ... while asking,

I pray that my frail words will
Steep into Your heart
So we can sip the cup of fellowship
Together.

Let the ribbon of Your love
Intermingle throughout my prayer,
And tie a lovely bow of encouragement there ... .

Help me ... to see ...
Your WEAVING
Instead of mine,
And make me wholly Thine.

Help me to digest the cup of joy and hope
To sustain me throughout the day.
Lead me ... O ... Blessed Saviour
By Thy Precious Hand ... .

The Underweaving of My Soul

Lord ... You see the underweaving
Of my soul.
You sometimes weave in scarlet,
And sometimes in gold,
And sometimes purple and of blue:
From this servant's heart an
Image woven of You.

I cannot comprehend the weaving
Of my Master's hand;
I know His ways and His thoughts
Are higher than I can understand.
After the darkness passes away,
There comes to me God's Shekinah Glory,
A radiance of His glorious hope.
It is then He weaves a majestic
Golden thread.

When I walk through the valleys
So dark ... with deep ravines,
I know ... my Lord is with me.
You are the unblemished "Lamb of God"
Whose life's atoning blood flowed.
It was then Your sacrificial
Thread of scarlet was woven.

Often in reverential awe my heart
Basks in the ethereal presence of my King.
It is then He weaves His Royal
Thread of purple.

Holy He came ... to save a world;

Blameless ... yet accused.
Divine Deity is engraven

Upon His golden crown.
He gave away Himself ... to redeem me
It was then He weaved the supremacy
Of the thread of blue ... .

Glory... to the King of Kings

I thank You, Lord,
That on Calvary's hill
Your love was scarlet;
Your love was real.
From Your lips You uttered my forgiveness;
From my sins You set me free:
You gave to me your Victory.

HALLELUJAH! What a Saviour!

Lord ... lift me higher than I've been before,
Higher to heaven's open door.
I cannot fathom Your wondrous grace
Until one day when I see You face to face.
I cannot comprehend Your
Miraculous love for me
'til in the glory of heaven I see Thee.

Glory ... to the King of kings!

Through It All

In my walk with Jesus
I may stumble ... I may fall,
But I know Jesus is with me
Through it all.

I can soar above my problems
Like an eagle;
I am so close to heaven
When on Jesus I call.

He knows my every trial;
He feels every pain;
And I know ... one day ... I'll gain
Heaven's fame.

His Spirit continually is with me;
His love embraces so dear,
I couldn't make it if ...
Jesus wasn't near.

From my eyes He dries
My every tear.
He holds me in His arms;
He calms all my fears.

Though ... the valley be dark,
And burdens cover my way,
I know ... Jesus walks with me.
By my side He will stay

Forever.

Again ... I Walk

Again ... I walk through the valley;
I sense the presence of my Lord so sweetly.
I focus on His compassionate face;
From His heart He gives me His infinite
Mercy and Grace.

Through the valley I have seen a glorious light,
For I know that Jesus walks before me.
He clears my difficult path,
And places a rose
Where the thorns grow.

I don't mind the valley anymore,
For Jesus and I are dearest friends;
He understands my pain
And I learn more of Him.

Precious name

Jewels of Red

It had been raining for days.
The strawberries glistened in rows of red
As they hung on the glossy green vines.
We found a lot of spoiled berries.
This reminded me of Christians
Who are true followers of Jesus
In this world today. We are washed
Through the blood of Jesus, and we
Become as jewels for His kingdom.
We must persevere in a troubled
World with sin (the spoils that
are all around us). When we go
Through the storms in our lives,
We know that Jesus is near.
With the berries as well as ourselves,
We know brighter days are just ahead.
We are God's jewels
That have been cleansed with the
Rains of the Holy Spirit, and redeemed,
We are ready to shine in the world
For spoiled berries. It's not how
Long the row we must harvest,
But how many berries (souls)
We can bring to God ... the True Vine.

A Light in the Window

Keep a light in the window for me,
Precious Father:
A light to guide – a light to follow.

Sometimes I may wander
Away from Your mercy and grace.

Search me, Precious Father;
Bring me home to where the radiance of Your eternal
Flame is burning.

Focus my eyes on the heavenly mansion on the hill;
Place Your nail – scarred hand over my heart
Where Your Divine Love is sealed.

Keep the eternal light burning,
Precious Father:
Keep it in the window of Your heart.
Keep Your arms ever reaching to forgive
And to guide me,
Where Your unconditional love so awesomely imparts.

*"Whom have I in heaven but thee? And there is none
upon earth that I desire beside thee. "
(Psalm 73:25, KJV)*

*When Daddy lay ill, during his final days, I could look
from our house to Mother and Dad s house on the hill.
In the darkness I could see the light in the window by
his bed. That light guided Daddy home, and one day I
shall see him again.
Hallelujah!*

I've Come Too Far to Turn Back

There's too much to gain
To turn back now.
My Lord will help me reach a higher plain ... .
I cannot lose the peace in my heart
For moments of unrest;
I cannot lose my sight of hope
While going through this test... .

I cannot walk away from God's love
And turn back to hate:
I've come too far to turn back.
God did not crucify worldly desires
For me to deny His pow'r ... .

He did not bring me through the valley
To turn back to miry clay;
He did not raise me above to be beneath.
He dwells within,
So I can rise above all things.
Peace, Love, Joy, and Hope He brings...
And so much more!
To the ones who walk uprightly.
God has brought me too far to turn back now.

*"For the LORD GOD is a sun and shield: the
LORD will give grace and glory: no good thing
Will he withhold from them that walk uprightly."
(Psalm 84:11 KJV)*

*"The righteous shall be glad in the LORD, and shall
trust in him and all the upright in heart shall glory."
(Psalm 64:10, KJV)*

Walking With Jesus

In my walk with Jesus
I may stumble ... I may fall,
But Jesus is there with me through it all.
I can soar above my problems like an eagle;
I feel so near to heaven
When on Jesus I call.
He knows my every trial;
He feels my every pain,
And I know ... one day heaven I'll gain.
His Spirit continually is with me;
His love embraces so dear:
I couldn't make it if Jesus wasn't near.
From my eyes ... He dries my every tear;
He holds me in His arms;
He calms my every fear.
Though the valley be dark and burdensome along the way,
Jesus is with me ... I know by my side He will stay.

Mary ... Behold Thy Son!!

Mary ... behold thy Son –
Upon His Divine shoulders weighed
All the sins of the world.
Jesus, our awesome Sacrifice,
There is no greater one.

HE WAS MAN – YET DIVINE.

Once Mary held sweet Jesus in her arms
With heart full of joy;
Now ... He has died a cruel death.
Again ... she holds Him only in her heart
With unquenchable pain:
Her own sweet Boy.

Soon ... sweet Mary will know the reason why
Her heart stood still that day ... .
The sorrow in her heart would
Soon be transformed to jubilee:
Hope of eternity-hope for you and for me.

Soon ... the remorse of that old rugged cross
Would be behind her,
When she beholds sweet Jesus in a glorified array.

PRAISE TO THE KING OF KINGS.

She will no longer ponder the deep things of God,
But look upon Him once again
As she did when Jesus was a little boy,
With eyes full of adoration:
For then sweet Mary ... will behold her resurrected Son!!

GLORY! HALLELUJAH! WHAT A SAVIOUR!

Be Thou My Vision

When the sky darkens
And the storm comes,
Help me, precious Father,
To see "Thy Light" beyond –

Be Thou my Vision.

When the thunder sounds
With Thy sacred clouds of rain
These tears cleanse my
Soul of its pain –

Be Thou my Vision.

Be Thou my Strength
In this time of weakness;
Thou hast not forsaken me,
But given me a cross
To weave into a crown.

Be Thou my Vision

You have not let me down,
But lifted me up;
You have not forsaken,
But have overflowed my cup.

Be Thou my Vision.

Through Your living Word,
I can conquer and banish the word of fear.
Through Your promises,
I can learn to walk.

Through my trials –
I have not been forsaken,
Because Thou hast loved me through.
I've come through to praise
Thy mighty pow'r –

Be Thou my Vision ...

Be ... Thou ... my ... Vision!

*"For what is our hope, or joy, or crown of rejoicing?
Are not even ye in the presence of our Lord Jesus
Christ at his coming? :For ye are our Glory and joy."
(1 Thessalonians 2:19, 20, KJV)*

The story behind
"BE THOU MY VISION"

This is a true story about a lovely young woman who
faithfully served her Lord, Jesus Christ. Her name
was Jill. One of the first times I talked to Jill was at
Norton's Hospital. I soon realized the tremendous
journey she was facing, and I also knew as we shared,
prayed, and wept together that I wanted to be there for
her in the midst of her struggles and her pain. I wanted
to help her carry her cross. Through the days of her
illness I shared with her many ways of
encouragement. I gave Jill all of myself through the
guidance of the Holy Spirit. God not only commands
us to "pray for one another," but to serve each other
through obedience and humility. This means, walking
with them through their trials, and when they grow
weary from their load, "to wash the dust from their
feet with the tears from our soul." In doing so, we are
true servants of our Lord Jesus Christ.

"Carry each other's burdens, and in this way
you will fulfill the law of Christ."
(Galatians 6:2 NJV)

Jill pressed through and won her supreme and heavenly prize when Jesus called her home on April 4, 2002. I began this poem to Jill, my beloved sister in Christ who is now on a higher plane, serving her Master. I'll share the part Jill commented on at one time. She remarked, "I am beginning to see the Light of Jesus." "When the sky darkens, and the storm comes ... Help me, precious Father, to see "Thy Light" beyond ... ."

"The sun will no more be your light by day, nor will
the brightness of the moon shine on you, for the
LORD will be your ever lasting light, and your God
will be your glory."
(Isaiah 60:19, NIV)

Teach Me To Fly

Teach me to fly –
Not on my own,
But by your side –

I trust You when I fall.
I know You will always be there:
You love me too much
To let me slip through Your hands.

Even in deep distress
You are leading me
Into a sacred place –
To seek only Your Holy Face.

You sift me like grains of sand –
I am like perfume to Your soul.

By faith I know
You, O Lord, direct my steps.

Through You my ways are safe and secure.

I've learned,
Tho' my eyes cannot see –
You watch over me
 With a Father's eyes.

"A *man's heart deviseth his way:*
but the LORD directeth his steps."
      (Proverbs 16:9, *KJV)*

Destined to walk
In His steps.

Heaven's Loft

O Lord, lift me up to a quiet place
In the sanctuary of Thy soul:
A place through the night
Where I can sing Your song –
And pray myself to sleep,

"Yet *the LORD will command his loving kindness in*
the daytime, and in the night his song shall be with
me, and my prayer unto the God of my life."
(Psalm 42:8, KJV)

O my Rock, in these ages
You hide my soul in Thy
Sustaining presence.
O Lord, You are my Refuge,
My Shelter,
My Rock on which I stand,
The Keeper of my soul
In the hollow of Thy hand
All the day long.

Thy Holy Raiment of Mercy
Covereth my soul;
Thy anointing grace
Refreshes my spirit
Like cool pools of water
Descending from heaven's
Upper chambers.

O Lord, how majestic is
Thy holy name.
You raise me up to lofty heights
To behold the grandeur of
Thy Glory.

I remember the loft in Daddy s barn. I had to climb the wooden ladder to get to the upper level. As it is with our spiritual walk, we must constantly seek after the Higher things and the wonders of God to experience the grandeur of His Glory.

My Daddy, Curtis Blackman

A Sacred Moment

We're sitting on the back
Porch of my soul:
Just my Lord and I –
How pleasant is His sanctuary
Of holy quietness.
I hear God whisper through the
Rhythm of the raindrops
Descending into the night.

He refreshes my soul
As He releases the busyness
Of my day into His care.

I can't remember when He's
Never come
With refreshment from His Spirit.
He has been always with me
With the rhythm of heaven's
Music:
To refresh – to renew
To repair – to restore.

My heart is clothed with
His peace;
I've felt His sweet Holy Presence,
And I desire to know Him
Superabundantly more.

*After a very busy day I walked out on our back porch
to be alone with God. It had been raining, and the
night stood still around me. The raindrops upon the
barn roof brought a soothing sound. They took me*

169

into His Holy Sanctuary, away from the busyness of this world. My greatest desire is to spend time alone with God, to hear the meditations from His soul, loving Him for who He is and for who I am when I am in His presence.

On the Wings of the Morning

O wings of the morning,
Faith's enduring song,
Many times the clouds conceal
The treasures found in our
Rainbows –
O faithful hand that rolls
Back the clouds as a scroll.

Why fret when God can look
Into your soul –
Ultimately, He has everything in
Control.

Oh, cometh sweet, sweet dawn.
As the morning harmonizes with
The song of His sacred quietness,
He calls me softly aside to walk
With Him –
A refreshing place of rest
Before
The day's demand
And
A place of restoration at
Day's end.

Oh, the sweet aroma of
Myrrh and frankincense –
Your holy presence –
Your quintessence.

Oh, glory to God in the Highest!
He calls me into His luminous Light
To walk by faith, and not through
My human eyes.

In His time, shuttles will cease
And the midnight hours come.

Amid His trump's resound –
Oh, may I, my dear soul
Be found
Ascending,
Safe and secure
On Heaven's Holy Ground –
Hallelujah!!

Whenever my morning life permits, I love spending time with God in the fresh moments of the dawn, and when the day comes to a holy hush over the earth. Only His saving grace can turn the storm clouds into light, and we frame it a miracle. Only God can turn the tide of time into eternity, for He is forever. One day our faith shall be made into the sight of heaven, when the trumpet sounds, and You take Your children home.

"We have also a more sure word of prophecy; whereunto ye do well that ye take heed as unto a light that shineth in a dark place, until the day dawn, and the day star arise in your hearts."
(2 Peter 1:19, KJV)

God takes us where we are – to be where He is –
Hallelujah!

In Thy Holy Sanctuary

O Living Water, everlasting:
Only You can satisfy our
Yearning souls.
You are our artesian well,
An ever-enduring spring –
Our Eternal King.

O Divine Essence,
Our prayers ascend heavenward
Like fragrant flowers placed
Before Thy Holy Chambers.

Let our voices exalt with
Loud refrain –
Before you, O my King.

Soul, prepare yourself before Him,
And raise
Your sweetest offering
With words of everlasting praise.

He treasures our prayers,
And in time we shall reap
The rewards of His fragrant
Blessings.

It's been so *wonderful to be in His presence. I am but
a soundless cymbal without Him. It is an honor to be
His pen flowing with His anointing. I owe everything I
am and everything I ever hope to be to You,* O *my King.*

*"To the end that my tongue and my heart and everything
glorious within me may sing praise to You and not be
silent. O Lord my God, I will give* thanks *to You for ever."
(Psalm 30:12, Amp.)*

173

His Tears Cleanse

God washes my soul with His tears.

A waterfall of His Great Mercy
Caresses my spirit,
Flowing down from the
Watersprings of Heaven.

In the undercurrent of my soul
He cleanseth me with
The tears from His eyes –
He brings me through the storms,
From the underneath to the upper side –
His fountain of strength eternally
Supplies –
He has never failed me.

He whispers in the whirlwind,
His prevailing power –
And upholds me in the veil of
This midnight hour –
O Lord, You are my
Eternal Watchtower.

*"I will say of the LORD, He is my refuge and my
fortress: my God; in him will I trust."
(Psalm 91:2, KJV)*

Jesus, My Encourager
MY STORY

How can a vessel of clay, such as we are, pour out to others when we ourselves are hurting, discouraged, or having a gray day? I am a vessel often touched by the infirmities of others. In reality, I love walking with the wounded. God has called me to be an encourager – a Barnabas. I am mindful of the pathways many people journey. I stand amazed, looking to my Lord for the answers found in His Holy Scriptures, our road map. I can see so much through God's Eyes. I am a warrior ready and willing to pour out myself for His cause, and always ready to learn from His Spirit superabundantly more. We are conquerors and overcomers through Christ *(1 John 4:4)*. God triumphs through us *(Psalm 147:3)*. Through my card ministry and phone calls, I encourage a lot of people in all walks of life. As I pour out to others, God supplies my needs as well. As a boomerang returns to its sender, God replenishes me.

Scripture reference*: Matthew 25:35, 36 (Amp). "For I was hungry and you gave Me food."* You gave me strength from you spirit and soul. You shared the bread of life with me. *"I was thirsty and you gave Me something to drink."* You gave me your encouragement when I needed it. You gave me a fresh cup of the Living Water in my times of drought from a well that never runs dry. *I was a stranger and you brought Me together with yourselves and welcomed and entertained and lodged Me."* In my times of need you came to my heart and took residence. You lifted me with Christ's love and understanding. With patience you walked me through my struggles. You gave me hope in times of despair. *"I was naked and you clothed Me."* You came and covered me several times with the garment of love. You clothed me with your faithful care. *"I was sick and you visited Me,"* with help and ministering care. *"I was in prison and you came to see Me."* Through sickness you found strength through God's Holy Scriptures. You found you are not alone behind the prison bars of this world. There are people who care. People like me! In God's goodness and mercy, I am Barnabas (your encourager). Remember, Paul says in Acts 20:32, *"Now I entrust you to God and His care."*

In His Own Time

Another day of Your mercy –
At Your command I see
Thy golden sunrise –
At Your altar my bended knee.

Another day of Thy grace –
Oh, what confidence to know
You walk with me,
Giving me Thy strength to face my day.

Oh, what consolation to know I can
Talk to You, anytime
Through the quintillion galaxies
Of space.

Crown Him – Crown Him – Lord of All

O King Eternal,
Thou who knows
All there is to know about me –
Can see my end from my beginning,
While looking into a single
Moment of time *(Psalm 90:4)* –

You have fashioned my life very
Intricately.

My Sovereign Glory

Oh, what Joy and Peace through our blessed
Redeemer
Who holds our souls
And preserves us
Through His Righteousness
(Psalm 66:9)

We may think we write our own chapter in the book of our life, when instead God has planned and ordained our days, and preserved them for His eternal glory. God designs an eternal legacy for us to leave behind. Our lives are woven into an everlasting impression of His great love with beautiful reflections of our Great God, Immanuel, our Lazarus, our Lamb of God who gave to us His greatest, most beautiful and priceless Sacrifice to fashion a living memorial in the hearts of those who are touched divinely throughout our lives.

In Him alone.

It Is the Presence

Oh, how I enjoy this sacred
Moment of time –
Just to pause
For a while,
And feel
The anointing
Of Your Spirit
Intermingle with mine –

Oh, to attain the mighty grandeur
Of Your strengthening
Power –
Oh, how hallowed Your "Holy Parousia,"
The "fullness of
Thy Presence."

Hallelujah! !

Many times You've pulled me
From my dark places
To comfort me.
In my times of feeling alone,
You draw me closer,
And You give me "Hope" to carry on" –

In so many ways
Your "Holy Light" scatters my "darkness,"
So as in embracing it,
You interweave my "darkness" with "Thy Light,"
And you bless me with Thy Holy
Easter Dawn –

Alleluia!!

Our lives are filled with many wonderful things, but nothing compares with being in the Holy Presence of our Lord. There's not a place He cannot fill – and there's not a need for which He cannot provide His sustaining Power. He takes us to places that we long to be.

> *"Thou wilt show me the path of life:*
> *Of joys there is full store –*
> *Before Thy face; at Thy right hand*
> *Are pleasures evermore –" (Psalm 16:11).*

Taken from a very old Bible hundreds of years old. These Psalms of David are in poetic form of these sacred writings.

To God Be the Glory!

The Valley of Baca (Tears)

I was torn at what to do in my valley of tears and sorrow. Some things seemed right, some uncertain. I know God was with me in it. He knows how to transform my "Valley of Sorrow" into "joy" –

Do you often feel you've been through a week's worth of circumstances, and it's only Tuesday? We can triumph through tragedy, no matter what the circumstances weigh in. God can use every experience in a positive way. In His Word He reminds us, "This, too, shall pass." It does, through His grace imparted. Through the revelation of our Master He equips us and helps us to transform others through to the process of "joy" through their mourning. God promises to never leave us. He is everywhere we need Him to be. What a Saviour! God does not waste our tears or pain. There is a purpose in everything, and He sees us through it all. Does it happen to you that some days you are numb to the world, and other days God gives you revelation on every side? How can we calculate all that? I believe it's the cares of this world that weigh on our spirits. Whether in "sorrow" or in "joy," the Lord will provide. When we shut the door behind us, and crawl up into His arms, He straightens out our crooked paths, as we bask in His Word and His glory.

Glory to the Lamb of God!

If Only To Lean

If only to lean
Amid earth's toils
And find my rest –
Upon my Saviour's breast –

If only to lean
While tired, yet pressing through –
As long as my Saviour walks with me
In all storms anew –

If only to lean
And know my Saviour is there –
Guiding my footsteps
Through my daily cares –

If only to lean
I shall press on –
For I know His Hand
Gracefully opens a scroll to a
Brighter dawn –

If only to lean –
O Blessed Assurance,
O Blessed Rock of these Ages!
I know my Saviour is always
With me –
If only I lean –
I know He will never let me fall.

A **Mother's Garden of Love**

*(In memory of Myrtle Stults, and for
daughters Rita and Betty, and son Bobby)*

Oh, how I remember
My precious mother, a godly woman,
And the gifts of her spirit she gave away.
She gave to me a bouquet
Of her everlasting love.
Oh, the many struggles she had to bear,
But for me, she was always there.

With her caring hands
She fashioned beautiful things;
They were, to me, stitched with golden threads.
To her family tree she added
A circle of friends;
The giving of herself possessed no end.

She loved to spend time in the garden.
I can envision her now,
Wearing an old straw hat, and in her hand a hoe.
She loved to plant seeds and watch
Them sprout and grow.

Now she is a gardener by the Master's side.
Heaven is a place of perpetual beauty
Where there is no more sorrow and no more strife.
There she is with her friends by the beautiful
Garden of eternal life.

When she grew weary from the toils here,
She would rest underneath a tree
Where she loved to sit in the swing.
The swing is idle now,
And the singing of the birds doesn't sound as sweet.

I miss Mother's encouraging words;
She taught me, as best as she knew,
The love of God, and the right things to do.
Mother, my precious pearl: oh, how I love her so!
Around my heart, I wear a priceless locket of her love,
Of the eternal values she gave to me:
They are more to me than things of fine gold.

A Glimpse Through the Veil

Some days
Life seems to quickly pass by –
So it can be with a
Glimpse of God's Glory.
We can miss it in the
Twinkling of an eye –

"Bless the LORD, O my soul!
O LORD my God, You are very great."
(Psalm 104:1a, NASB)

The luminous orange clouds
Appeared
In supernal ecstasy,
Rejoicing
With the misty periwinkle blue –
"You are clothed with splendor and majesty." (v. 16)

The black silhouette of the trees
Were drenched with autumn rain,
Creating a majestic panorama view –
"Covering Yourself with light as with a cloak.
Stretching out heaven like, a tent curtain." (v. 2)

The world is Your palette,
And at Your command
You call forth Thy firmament,
And arrange the clouds with
Thy Miraculous Hand –
"Praise the LORD, O my soul, all my inmost being,
praise his holy name."
(Psalm 103:1, NIV)

In my senior years it seems life passes more quickly and becomes much too repetitious. At times our lives are filled with too many things. I am so thankful there's pardon in God's bosom. I feel safe there in His care. His creation speaks to many in different ways. I am reminded daily that He is walking by my side. I am claiming Philippians 3:10 as my new year's resolution, to know my Saviour in a greater capacity, and grow in His Grace and Compassion and Empathy for others. His creations will always inspire me. He calls me aside to relax and enjoy Him.

To God be the Glory!

Our Father Knows

Do you sometimes feel you are
On the road to Gethsemane –
And your tears flow,
And your heart is overwhelmed with pain?

... Our Father Knows ... .

I felt His wonderful peace as
He stood next to me –
He sees each tear,
And feels the sadness
that pain has brought.
He walks with you,
And will never leave you
To carry it alone.
Oh, He will help you face –
That tomorrow,

And lift you from beneath
To the upper side of His Sustaining Grace –

Blessed Assurance.

Our Father's mercy overflows.
As He is sovereign on sorrow's path,
He wants you to know –
He is the Keeper of your heart
Forever and always
In the bosom of His soul –

"Those that are broken in their heart
And grieved in their minds –
He healeth, and their painful wounds
He tenderly upbinds."
(Psalm 147:3,4)

Scripture taken from a very old Bible. Only God has the power and wisdom to turn the ancient pages of time. To Him who holds the universe in His Hands. I trust Him to hold me through His majestic wisdom.

Our Refuge of Hope

Holding Me Within the Vale

Lord, Thou comest ever so sweetly in
The midst of this shaded vale.
You are holding me in Your arms;
Your strength embraces me;
Thy promises never fail.

Alleluia!

Thy rod and Thy staff, they comfort me
In the shadows of this valley.
Oh, lead me beside the still water!
Oh, hearken my soul!
Thou cometh to refresh my spirit
Where I will thirst no more.

You caress my soul
Nearer Heaven's Heights.
I know I am led in the Holy Presence
Of Thy Sacred Light.

When things begin to fail me,
Through Your eyes I must learn to see.
I know ... this life is perishable,
And I must release it from my soul.
I hope to attain it through Your grace
And Your Divine mercy, and
Someday reach the fullness
Of Your love ... .

Jesus – Just the Mention of That Name

[On October 7, I had the privilege of speaking at a women's ministry in New Albany. Does *Jesus'* glory shine through you?]

> *"Therefore, if anyone is in Christ, he is a new creation; the old has gone, the new has come!"*
> *(2 Corinthians 5:17, NIV)*

Jesus – just the mention of that name! (At this time, I felt the ushering of the presence of the Holy Spirit.)

> *"I have been crucified with Christ and I no longer live, but Christ lives in me. The life I live in the body, I live by faith in the Son of God who loved me and gave himself for me."*
> *(Galatians 2:20, NIV)*

Jesus – gave Himself on the cross of Calvary for me. He died so I can live. *Jesus* gave away His love and His life on the cross to save us.

> *"For God so loved you and me He gave us His only Son – The very best He had to offer, that whosoever believes in Him shall not perish but have everlasting life in Him."*
> *(John 3:16)*

    Jesus – just the mention of that wonderful name can calm the wildest storm, can set the prisoner free of loneliness, discouragement, and unworthiness.
    Jesus –the Lily of the Valley, the sweet fragrance that fills every room in our hearts.
    Jesus – our Rose of Sharon blooming in the desert when life is hard and difficult.

Jesus – our Good Shepherd that guides our footsteps over the thorns and thistles in our lives. He leads His children to safety.

Jesus – just the mention of that name can calm the ships of our souls when our sails are tattered from the storms in our lives. He picks up the pieces that pain has scattered, and molds them back together, making them whole in body and in spirit.

Jesus – just the mention of that awesome name, through the breath of my spirit is an honor and a privilege. He calls me His friend and daughter of His Heavenly Kingdom.

Jesus – just the mention of that awesome name, sent His "power through me." In April 2004 I experienced an awesome cleansing of my spirit. He cleansed out the ugly past that Satan caused me to harbor. It was fast and complete. I felt the Hand of God and power go into my soul, and pull out the dark, ugly sin. I was set free, much like the mighty eagle soaring closer to the heart of God and His heaven.

Jesus – just the mention of His wonderful, marvelous name. Several months ago, I witnessed His mighty and reverent power while visiting a shut-in. As I stepped inside on her porch I encountered One so wonderful, so powerful, that was waiting for me. I felt like falling on my knees before His Holy Presence. He drew me closer to Him. He was so awesome! So beautiful! So glorious!

Jesus – just the mention of such an awesome name! My Saviour has brought me through such a siege of pain. He has been with me, encouraged me, beckoned me to lean on Him (and lean I did so much, so hard). I had some very difficult days, but He was always by my side. He never will let us walk alone, and we never need to, because He is right in step with us. He knows all about our lives. He knows the things we go through every minute of every day. And He wants to be our Saviour and our Friend. He wants to embrace us and never let us go.

Jesus – just the mention of that name! Many years ago when our children were younger I had spent a very trying day. My burden was heavy. I remember praying and asking God, "Why?" He gave me a scripture as His answer, as His assurance for me all the days of the rest of my life. He audibly spoke, "*... I am with you always" (Matthew 28:20a, NIV).* His voice was calming me: His voice of assurance. His Spirit is always with me: He will never leave me nor forsake me. He has promised. Many are His promises. He promises to save us, to free us, to give to us eternal life with Him through His blood that was shed only by Him and only through Him on Calvary's cross. Lay up your heavenly treasures today: not on this earth, but for that Heavenly Kingdom. In heaven treasures are eternal.

"Do not store up for yourselves treasures on earth, where moth and rust destroy, and where thieves break in and steal. But store up for yourselves treasures in heaven."
(Matthew 6:19, 20a, NIV)

"But we have this treasure in jars of clay to show that this all-surpassing power is from God and not from us."
(2 Corinthians 4: 7, NIV)

We are "hard pressed," on every side, but not "crushed"; "perplexed," but not in "despair"; "persecuted," but not

192

"abandoned." Jesus' Spirit lives in these jars of clay. His power is in us, overcoming the difficulties and despair.

"I can do everything through him who gives me strength."
(Philippians 4:13, NIV)

Jesus does "empower" us to do great and mighty things through Him, bringing Him the glory, only and always.

"You show that you are a letter from Christ, the result of our ministry, written not with ink but with the Spirit of the living God not on tablets of stone but on tablets of human hearts."

(2 Corinthians 3:3, NIV)

Amen.

Autumn's October

"To everything there is a season; and a time for every matter or purpose under heaven: A time to be born and a time to die, a time to plant and a time to pluck up what is planted ... A time to weep and a time to laugh, a time to mourn and a time to dance."
(Eclesiastes 3:1-4, Amp.)

Autumn leaves are gracefully
Hanging in droplets of orange,
Crimson, and gold.

As autumn's sweet voice I behold ...

The leaves begin to fall,
Cascading to the ground.
The trees now appear barren
As they become as black
Silhouettes standing tall ... .

The time to sow has passed ... .
Now a season of sorrow fills the air:
A time to weep and a time to mourn
As our dear daddy left us.
I will never forget
God's Glory I saw that day –
Through
an autumn's sunset
When our daddy went away.

Daddy, I miss you.
August 27, 1916 - October 14, 1999

The "Sweet Hour of Prayer" is a tender song for me.
Daddy and I prayed together often.

Prayer

I have heard your prayers
And seen your tears –
And felt your doubts and fears.

Know in your times of persecution
I will hear your cries –
And wipe the tears from your
Swollen eyes.

Sometimes My answer is, "Not now,"
And waiting, I know, is hard to do –

But I have a plan and a purpose.
You will have to trust in Me as I trust in you.

You need not worry
About anything,
For I, your Heavenly Father,
Who cares for the sparrows in the sky
And the flower of the field,
I promise to hold you, too.
I promise "I will."

I know you will ask for forgiveness
And patience, too –
And you want to be more like Me;
I will help you through.
You are a blessing, child,
And I your Beloved King.
You can trust Me with your life;
I am all you will ever need.

I gleaned this poem from a United Methodist Women's
Retreat entitled "What Happens When Women Pray,"
at Spring Mill Inn, October 26, 27, 2007. There were
eight women who attended from our church. We all
had a great time!

Cara's Miracle

A little angel came knocking
On heaven's door
To plead her heart before
The King (of Glory).
He listened with great mercy
And compassion.

While the promise of healing
To her ears came,
He shared with her a vision
When Cara would be made well.
He said it would take a little time.
This sweet little girl,

Heaven's Pearl:

Many carried her fervently
In prayer for her recovery.

The miracle came,
As seen through her eyes:
The vision as told by her King.

She is now able to do normal things
Like going to school
As she grows stronger.
A wheel chair is her only companion for now.
Someday Cara will walk,
And God will show her how.

I learned about Cara, who was stricken with leukemia from friends whom I met and lodged in their home while doing *missions in King City, California, in 1997 with Janet Rae. Cara lived in Franklin, Indiana. Cara is now well. Praise God!*

Yes, Cara, Jesus still performs miracles today as He did nearly 2000 years ago. His miracles amaze me!

His Unfailing Love

Often God takes me by my hand
And leads me through to His promises.
I hear His reassuring voice
As I journey with Him
Through the valleys so dim –
I go, but not by choice,
And sure again,
I find the answer:
It's always in Him.

In this world of struggles and despair
I am able to walk through
With His strong arms underneath, lifting me
Into the realm of His sweet peace:
Nothing here can compare.
Jesus is always where I am
In my busyness.

My spirit requires a secret place
Where I meet with my Lord
To draw from His unending strength
And His unfailing grace
From His artesian well, everlasting.
He has given me nothing else
But the best of Himself,
And He's all we need.

"And my God will meet all your needs according to
his glorious riches in Christ Jesus."
(Philippians 4:19, NIV)

A Light Unto My Path

He who holds us in the
Palm of His hands
Will also be my everlasting Light
Upon this unknown pathway.
Your comforting presence

Sustains me
In this hour.

"Thy word is a lamp unto my feet ... ."
(Psalm 119:105 KJV)

I cannot fathom Your intricate design
And Your Divine weaving.
Taken are threads
From a stormy trial,
And those gathered from rays
Of revelation light.
Woven is a garment
Of Your Eternal Presence of Peace and Love
Graced about my spirit and soul,
Enabling me to face
These uncertain hours and days –

"... and a light unto my path."
(Psalm 119:105, KJV)

O Love Divine –
The embrace of your never-failing
Hand in mine –
Gives me strength through
This difficult time –
There's never a cloud of mystery
That does not have its
Divine purpose,

Nor a sunny blue sky that
Does not know its destination
To lighten a heavy load –
O Radiant Light Divine,
Thou hast given unto me
More of Thyself
As a Lamplight unto my soul.

My mother spent time in the ER, ICU, and TCU. Much like the monitors that tell us all our vitals, God also gives us His monitoring skills through His promises and presence. He is constantly teaching us His ways through life experiences and His Holy Scriptures. " ... I am with you always" (Matthew 28:20a, NIV). I will forever and always lean on this promise, as I do so many others. I received this promise while also going through another difficult time. I hold it dearly to my heart, and it always stands out for me to grasp readily, and apply in my time of need. Our God is a Munificent Creator. He gives with great generosity.

O Precious Promises.

Holy Morning's Light

My own sweet mommy,
Hardships to endure:
To God and I you are so very precious;
His love is steadfast and sure.

When your valleys are so hard and long,
God's arms will embrace;
He is our Refuge and Strength:
In His arms...a safe place.

No matter the burdens you carried,
By your faith you did stand,
For you are never alone
When Jesus holds your hand.

The storm clouds may gather,
And comes the dreaded night,
But we know Jesus goes before you.

His Holy Presence
    guides;
Oh...His Holy Morning
    Light!

*"Those who sow in
Tears shall reap in joy."
(Psalm 126:5, NIV)*

A Vision of the Divine

I marvel at Your purple Majesty:
Your fiery orange
And Your luminous turquoise
Supervenes –
Unforeseen –
Oh, how glorious
Thy awesome splendor
Caused me to stand still
In the presence of Your creation.

Thy K-i-n-g-d-o-m come,
Thy W-i-l-l be done,
On E-a-r-t-h as it is in
H-e-a-v-e-n.

The sunrise is just a glimpse
Of Your glory
In that celestial city.
Even the grandeur of all sunrises
In the world
Cannot compare –
To the magniloquent brilliancy
That's up there.

For T-h-i-n-e is the
K-i-n-g-d-o-m
And the
P-o-w-e-r
And the
G-l-o-r-y

F-o-r-e-v-e-r
A-m-e-n.

God's Glorious sunrise brought me to my feet. I soon became immersed into its beauty. I stood in His Presence, exalting His Holy Name. It seemed like a short time when the sky turned to gray and eventually rain began to fall. His presence through that sunrise comforted me all day long. Our one and only true God personally promised that He will never leave us or forsake us (Hebrews 13:5, Matthew 28:20). Mother and I often prayed the Lord's Prayer. *It gave us a personal assurance to know He cares for us, and provides us with His sustaining grace and faithful guidelines to live abundantly for Him (Matthew 6:9-13). Are we anticipating the soon-coming Kings appearance in the Eastern sky? His presence will draw us to Him, as the sunrise did for me that glorious dawn.*

The Lord Is My Shepherd

Often the Holy Spirit calls me
"Beside the still waters."
He nudges me to stop and meditate

On His living words, and

Bask in the warmth of
His Holy Presence.

"He maketh me to lie down in green pastures:
He leadeth me beside the still waters.
He restoreth my soul he leadeth me in the paths
of righteousness for his name's sake."
(Psalm 23:2, 3 KJV)

About the Author

Visual poetic artist, Anita Karan, was born in 1943 near Elizabeth, Indiana. Her mother shared that she was born in an old farmhouse - just a hop, skip and a jump down the road, known as the old O'Bannon Farmhouse. Anita's Aunt Phyllis Blackman (now deceased) assisted in her birth. She has a younger brother, Gerald born in 1945.

Anita was married in her childhood church, The Bethesda UMC. She remembers the women scrubbing the old wooden floors at the entrance. Her small church was brimming with friends and family as Anita Karan Blackman and George Denzil Bube were united in marriage November 27, 1965. Rev. Wilbur Doan (pastor of the church at the time, now deceased), officiated.

Their firstborn was a son, Karl Duane, born in 1966. Their second child, daughter Teresa Karen, was born just three years later in 1969. They now have four grandchildren and two step-grandchildren.

As she looks back on that day, almost 48 years that seems to Anita like yesterday, having both sets of their parents present was the best gift of all. When we are young and full of plans we don't always realize how blessed we are.

Anita began to feel inspired by God in the late 1950's. She recalls walking on pathways through a neighbor's woods and digging up wildflowers and ferns as the presence of God surrounded her. She remembers the cow paths on the farm that led through the sassafras trees to the pond. Anita loved pathways not realizing at the time that God would lead her on His Glorious pathway. Her beloved mother who recently made her transition to Heaven to join hands with her Daddy has inspired her greatly and made the spiritual impact she carries in her heart today.

In Anita's second book (coming soon), *"Extracting the Precious Things"* [ref: Jeremiah 15:19 NASV] will portray within its pages loving tribute to her Mother and Daddy. Anita remembers purchasing a Layman's Encyclopedia from a traveling salesman and learning from Biblical mail order studies while yet at home with her Mother and Daddy on the farm.

For several years Anita has enjoyed writing a newspaper column for the Corydon Democrat, a local community newspaper, under the title of *"Northeast Posey."* She shares her own life, as well as nature, church happenings, world news and inspirations. Anita enjoys her card ministry (and phone ministry) encouraging people through her poetry and Biblical inspirations. Many have shared that they, "received their cards just when they needed the encouragement."

Anita's farm life inspired the title of her ministry: *"Eternal Seeds Outreach Ministry."* She feels she was entrusted by God to tell others "His story." Her aim is to glorify God and for Him alone "to be exalted." Her poems have become the voice of her own soul as prayers unto her Lord and Savior.

For spiritual ministry engagements please contact me at:

Eternal Seeds Outreach Ministry
Anita K. Bube
3700 N. Hwy 11 S.E.
Elizabeth, IN 47117
812-969-9000
Email: anita_k_bube@yahoo.com

Additional copies available directly on-line at: createspace.com/4184072

www.ingramcontent.com/pod-product-compliance
Lightning Source LLC
Chambersburg PA
CBHW022006090426
42741CB00007B/912